Johnny Depp

Other books in the People in the News series:

Maya Angelou
Tyra Banks
David Beckham
Beyoncé
Sandra Bullock
Fidel Castro
Kelly Clarkson
Hillary Clinton
Miley Cyrus
Ellen Degeneres
Leonardo DiCaprio
Hilary Duff
Zac Efron
Brett Favre
50 Cent
Al Gore
Tony Hawk
Salma Hayek
LeBron James
Jay-Z
Derek Jeter
Steve Jobs
Dwayne Johnson
Angelina Jolie
Jonas Brothers
Kim Jong II
Hamid Karzai
Coretta Scott King
Ashton Kutcher
Lady Gaga

George Lopez
Bernie Madoff
Tobey Maguire
Eli Manning
John McCain
Barack Obama
Michelle Obama
Danica Patrick
Nancy Pelosi
Tyler Perry
Michael Phelps
Queen Latifah
Daniel Radcliffe
Condoleezza Rice
Rihanna
Alex Rodriguez
J.K. Rowling
Shakira
Tupac Shakur
Will Smith
Sonia Sotomayor
Gwen Stefani
Ben Stiller
Hilary Swank
Justin Timberlake
Usher
Denzel Washington
Serena Williams
Oprah Winfrey

Johnny Depp

by John Grabowski

LUCENT BOOKS
A part of Gale, Cengage Learning

GALE
CENGAGE Learning™

Detroit • New York • San Francisco • New Haven, Conn • Waterville, Maine • London

© 2011 Gale, Cengage Learning

LIBRARY OF CONGRESS CATALOGING-IN-PUBLICATION DATA

Grabowski, John.
  Johnny Depp / by John Grabowski.
      p. cm. -- (People in the news)
  Includes bibliographical references and index.
  ISBN 978-1-4205-0292-3 (hardcover)
  1. Depp, Johnny. 2. Motion picture actors and actresses--United States--
Biography. I. Title.
  PN2287.D39G725 2011
  791.4302'8092--dc22
  [B]

                                                                  2011003417

Lucent Books
27500 Drake Rd
Farmington Hills MI 48331

ISBN-13: 978-1-4205-0292-3
ISBN-10: 1-4205-0292-1

Printed in the United States of America
1 2 3 4 5 6 7 15 14 13 12 11
Printed by Bang Printing, Brainerd, MN, 1st Ptg., 04/2011

Contents

Fame and celebrity are alluring. People are drawn to those who walk in fame's spotlight, whether they are known for great accomplishments or for notorious deeds. The lives of the famous pique public interest and attract attention, perhaps because their experiences seem in some ways so different from, yet in other ways so similar to, our own.

Newspapers, magazines, and television regularly capitalize on this fascination with celebrity by running profiles of famous people. For example, television programs such as *Entertainment Tonight* devote all their programming to stories about entertainment and entertainers. Magazines such as *People* fill their pages with stories of the private lives of famous people. Even newspapers, newsmagazines, and television news frequently delve into the lives of well-known personalities. Despite the number of articles and programs, few provide more than a superficial glimpse at their subjects.

Lucent's People in the News series offers young readers a deeper look into the lives of today's newsmakers, the influences that have shaped them, and the impact they have had in their fields of endeavor and on other people's lives. The subjects of the series hail from many disciplines and walks of life. They include authors, musicians, athletes, political leaders, entertainers, entrepreneurs, and others who have made a mark on modern life and who, in many cases, will continue to do so for years to come.

These biographies are more than factual chronicles. Each book emphasizes the contributions, accomplishments, or deeds that have brought fame or notoriety to the individual and shows how that person has influenced modern life. Authors portray their subjects in a realistic, unsentimental light. For example, Bill Gates – the cofounder and chief executive officer of the software giant Microsoft – has been instrumental in making personal computers the most vital tool of the modern age. Few dispute his business savvy, his perseverance, or his technical expertise, yet critics say he is ruthless in his dealings with competitors and driven more by his desire to maintain Microsoft's dominance in the computer industry than by an interest in furthering technology.

In these books, young readers will encounter inspiring stories about real people who achieved success despite enormous obstacles. Oprah Winfrey – the most powerful, most watched, and wealthiest woman on television today – spent the first six years of her life in the care of her grandparents while her unwed mother sought work and a better life elsewhere. Her adolescence was colored by rape, pregnancy at age fourteen, and sexual abuse.

Each author documents and supports his or her work with an array of primary and secondary source quotations taken from diaries, letters, speeches, and interviews. All quotes are footnoted to show readers exactly how and where biographers derive their information and provide guidance for further research. The quotations enliven the text by giving readers eyewitness views of the life and accomplishments of each person covered in the People in the News series.

In addition, each book in the series includes photographs, annotated bibliographies, timelines, and comprehensive indexes. For both the casual reader and the student researcher, the People in the News series offers insight into the lives of today's newsmakers – people who shape the way we live, work, and play in the modern age.

The Reluctant Superstar

Johnny Depp never intended to be a movie star. His goal in life as a young boy in Miramar, Florida, was to be a musician in a rock band, like KISS, Aerosmith, or Alice Cooper. It was only by a quirk of fate that Depp became an actor.

Depp's career has taken many turns along the way. There have been rough times, both professionally and in his personal life. He has had a reputation as a wild man, a bad boy, and a rebel. His temper got him in trouble with the law on several occasions.

Through it all, however, he has managed to persevere. He has held true to his beliefs in his professional life. Depp only accepted roles that interested him rather than those that would advance his career. Says his good friend, director Tim Burton, "He's always been true to who he is. He's never been ruled by money, or by what people think he should or shouldn't do."[1]

Megastar Status

Depp's work has won him worldwide praise. He prefers playing eccentric characters rather than the leading-man roles of actors such as Tom Cruise. Since 2003, however, he has become a red-hot property following his portrayal of pirate Jack Sparrow in Disney's *Pirates of the Caribbean: The Curse of the Black Pearl* .

Johnny Depp is one of the most versatile actors in Hollywood.

Depp was not the only actor considered for the part of Sparrow. Michael Keaton, Jim Carrey, and Christopher Walken were all considered before Depp was chosen. Disney executives questioned his interpretation of the character, but Depp stuck to his convictions and the movie-going public proved him right.

Fans flocked to the movie in record numbers. The film grossed more than $650 million worldwide. Together with its two sequels, the Pirates franchise has grossed approximately $3 billion worldwide. It has sparked renewed interest in the swashbuckling raiders of the high seas and brought Depp several awards for his acting.

Success and Fulfillment

Many of his peers consider him the best actor of his generation. Despite the awards and honors that have come his way, however, he always remembers the fans who pay to see his movies. Says Depp,

> The only reason I'm here is because of them. The only reason that I still get jobs is because of those people out there who are hanging out in the street waiting to get something signed or to say, 'Hi,' and shake your hand. So if they want me to come and say, 'Hi,' I am more than happy to say, 'Hi,' and I'll do it for as long as they want me to do it. They're keeping me alive. They're keeping my kiddies fed so they're the boss as far as I'm concerned.[2]

In his personal life, Depp had one failed marriage at a young age, followed by several engagements that ultimately dissolved. Eventually, he met French singer and actress Vanessa Paradis. They fell in love and settled down to live in France, where they raise their two children, Lily-Rose and Jack. As far as Depp is concerned, having a family has made his life complete.

Chapter 1

Searching for Direction

Johnny Depp sometimes refers to his temper as his "hillbilly rage."[3] This is a reference to his upbringing in Owensboro, Kentucky. As a troubled youth, he had a long road to travel to pull his life together and give it direction.

"Barbecue Capital of the World"

John Christopher Depp II was born on June 9, 1963, to Betty Sue Palmer and John Christopher Depp Sr. He was the youngest of four children in the family. The two oldest—Dan and Debbi —were from Betty Sue's previous marriage. Daughter Christie was the couple's first child, born 2½ years before Johnny. Johnny's heritage was a mixture of German, Irish, and Cherokee Indian.

The Depps lived in Owensboro, Kentucky, known by locals as "the barbecue capital of the world." Johnny's father was a city engineer for the town. His mom worked as a waitress at a local restaurant. One of Johnny's early memories was of his mother counting her tips at the end of the night. With both parents contributing to the finances, the Depps lived what Johnny believed was a more or less average, middle-class, blue-collar, American existence.

Johnny was not a typical, average child. Even at an early age, he showed an independent spirit, great imagination, and flair for the unusual. "I made odd noises as a child," he recalled. "Just did weird things, like turn off light switches twice. I think my parents thought I had Tourette's syndrome."[4] His siblings —whom he has remained close to through the years—gave him nicknames, such as "Johnny Dip" and "Deppity Dog."

Johnny was very close to his maternal grandfather, whom he called Paw Paw. His grandparents owned a tobacco farm in Frankfort, Kentucky, about a hundred miles away. Johnny and Paw Paw would spend time together picking tobacco or just talking. When his grandfather died in 1970, Johnny was greatly affected. "Somehow I believe that he's around," said Johnny. "I believe in ghosts... I'm sure my Paw Paw is around—guiding, watching."[5]

Acting Out

Shortly after his grandfather's death, Johnny and his family moved to Miramar, Florida. They lived in motels for a year until his father found regular work. By that time, Johnny had become aware of strained relations between his parents. "I remember my parents fighting all the time and I remember my brother and sisters and I wondering what would happen—if they did split up, who would go with whom?"[6]

Johnny's behavior became more erratic. He began smoking at the age of twelve, followed soon after by drinking and taking assorted drugs. He took part in vandalism and petty theft, earning a reputation as a troubled youngster. Says Johnny:

> I experimented with drugs and I experimented with everything that little boys do. Vandalism, throwing eggs at cars, breaking and entering schools and destroying a room. But I finally got to a point where I looked around and said, 'This is not getting me anywhere. I'm stagnating with these guys.' They were getting drunk and [taking drugs] every weekend. I got out.[7]

Sal Jenco

While Johnny Depp was growing up in Florida, his closest friend was Sal Jenco. The bond between the two was very strong. Sal had a difficult home life and eventually decided to move out on his own. He did not have much money, however, and was forced to live out of his run-down 1967 Chevrolet Impala for a while. In a show of loyalty to his friend, Depp lived in the car with him. He later said they survived by stealing sandwiches and drinks from a local 7/11.

After Depp became a star on *21 Jump Street*, Sal visited him on the set in Vancouver. He managed to impress the show's producers and was offered a role in the show. He played the part of janitor Salvatore "Blowfish" Banducci.

In later years, Sal managed Depp's nightclub, The Viper Room. He played drums with P, a band Depp formed together with Bill Carter and Gibby Haynes in 1993, and also had minor roles in two of Depp's films, *Arizona Dream* and *Donnie Brasco*.

Johnny was not a good student. He hated the rules and regulations he was forced to follow in school and began to rebel in various ways. When he was fifteen, he thought a female teacher was trying to embarrass him in front of the class. As he turned away, he dropped his pants and mooned her. The incident led to his being suspended for two weeks. It was becoming obvious to Johnny that he was not meant for school. By now, his interests had turned in another direction.

A Passion for Music

One of Johnny's uncles was an evangelical preacher, and Johnny occasionally went to his revivals. As part of the proceedings, a gospel rock band that included a couple of Johnny's cousins would perform. For Johnny, it was love at first sight. "My cousins'

Depp's mother bought him his first guitar, which he taught himself how to play.

band was the first time I had ever seen an electric guitar," he said, "and I became instantly hooked."[8]

Johnny talked his mom into buying him a Decca electric guitar for $25. He became obsessed with the instrument. He recalls:

This is horrible, the first thing I did was steal a Mel Bay chord book. I went to this store, stuffed it down my pants and walked out. It had pictures—that's why I needed it so badly, because it was immediate gratification. If I could match those photographs, then I was golden. I conquered it in days. I locked the bedroom door, didn't leave, and taught myself how to play chords. I started learning songs by ear.[9]

Eventually he felt good enough about his music to begin playing in garage bands. The first one was named Flame.

One of Johnny's favorite bands at the time was KISS. His fixation with the group almost had tragic consequences. Says Johnny:

I was maybe 12 and me and this friend put a t-shirt on the end of a broom handle, soaked it in gasoline and lit it. Then I put gasoline in my mouth and breathed fire like Gene Simmons of KISS. Only it set my face on fire; I was running down the street with my face on fire. My mom obviously was going to see that my face was all burned up, so I lied completely. I said we were shooting fireworks off and one went off in my face…The fireworks story was easier for her and me; and she bought it, bless her heart.[10]

The Family Splits

Around that same time, his mother and father divorced. Johnny remembered how the breakup affected his mother. "Her life as she had known it for 20 years was over," he said. "Her partner, her husband, her best friend, her lover, had just left her. I felt crushed that he had left, but when you're faced with something like that, it's amazing how much abuse the human mind and heart can take. You just get past what you need to get past."[11]

Johnny, his sister Christie, and his brother Dan stayed with his mother, while his half-sister Debbie moved to Hallandale, Florida, to live with his father. Despite the breakup, Johnny remained fiercely loyal to both his parents. "When my parents split up was when I think I realized these are the most important people in my

Johnny Depp's mom, Betty Sue, (left) accompanied her famous son to the Academy Awards in 2004.

life," he said, "and you know, I'd die for these people."[12]

Although he was the youngest one in the family, Johnny became responsible for picking up the weekly child support check at his father's office. He also took it upon himself to help his mother cope with the emotional scars left by a second failed marriage. At the same time, he continued to follow his dream of a career in music.

The Kids

By the time Depp was sixteen, he had decided to drop out of school. He reconsidered his decision, however, and went back a couple weeks later. Surprisingly, the dean at the school discouraged him from returning. Depp recalled, "He said, 'Johnny, we don't want you to come back'...it was really sweet, actually. He said, 'I know that you have this music thing...I think you should run with it...that's your passion, you should go with that.'"[13]

Depp directed all his energy into playing guitar with his new band, The Kids. The band started out slowly, playing cover songs

As a teenager, Depp played in the band The Kids, seen here performing a reunion show in 2008.

at local clubs. They eventually began performing their own material and started opening for bigger bands like the Talking Heads, the Pretenders, and the B-52s. Depp recalled, "I played rock 'n' roll clubs in Florida. I was underage, but they would let me come in the back door to play, and then I'd have to leave after the first set. That's how I made a living."[14]

Lori Anne Allison

One of the other members of The Kids had a friend who was a makeup artist. Depp was introduced to the girl, whose name was Lori Anne Allison. Lori Anne was twenty-five—five years older than Depp. Despite the age difference, there was an immediate attraction between the two.

After a brief courtship, Depp and Lori Anne were married on

Music Videos

Johnny Depp has appeared in a number of music videos, beginning in 1991 with "Into The Great Wide Open," by Tom Petty and The Heartbreakers. Since then, he has also been seen in the Lemonheads' "It's a Shame About Ray" (1992), Shane MacGowan's "That Woman's Got Me Drinking" (1994), Johnny Cash's "God's Gonna Cut You Down" (2006), and Babybird's "Unlovable" (2009). He has also directed and appeared in several of his girlfriend Vanessa's videos.

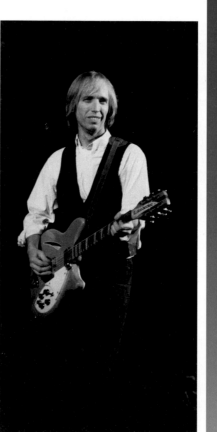

Depp appeared in a number of music videos, including Tom Petty and the Heartbreakers' "Into The Great Wide Open."

December 24, 1983. Depp later recalled, "I was married when I was twenty. It was a strong bond with someone but I can't necessarily say I was *in love*. That's something that comes around once…maybe twice if you're lucky. And I don't know that I experienced that…before I turned 30."[15]

California Calls

The Kids had become very popular in the South Florida area. The band's attempts to secure a record deal, however, were unsuccessful. The group decided to seek fame and fortune out west. They headed to California and settled in Los Angeles. In an attempt at a new start, the band changed its name to Six Gun Method.

Unfortunately, hundreds of other bands had the same plan. Said Depp, "There were so many bands it was impossible to make any money. So we all got side jobs. We used to sell ads over the telephone. Telemarketing. We got $100 a week. We had to rip people off. … It was horrible."[16]

The band continued to open for such acts as Billy Idol, the Bus Boys, and Iggy Pop, but dreams of rock stardom were beginning to fade. Depp eventually quit the band. The struggle had also taken a toll on his marriage. "I had the right intentions," said Depp, "but the wrong timing—and the wrong person…It wasn't working out, so we took care of it."[17] Depp and Lori Anne divorced in 1985.

A New Direction

Prior to their breakup, Lori Anne had introduced Depp to a friend of hers—a young actor by the name of Nicolas Cage. Cage came from a strong cinematic background. His uncle was director and producer Francis Ford Coppola, and his aunt, actress Talia Shire. He had recently appeared in his uncle's 1983 film, *Rumble Fish*.

Cage learned that Depp's music career had apparently reached a dead end. He knew Depp was looking for work and suggested he try his hand at acting. Cage introduced him to his agent, who

Depp's (far right) first acting role was in the 1984 movie A Nightmare on Elm Street.

told him about an open-call audition for a new horror film by director Wes Craven. The film was *A Nightmare on Elm Street*. Depp decided to try out for the part of Glen Lantz. Recalled Depp, "Glen was described as this big blond surfer jock type and here I was, this little scrawny, pale little guy with long dark hair starched to death with five-day old hairspray."[18]

Despite not fitting Craven's image of the character, Depp still made quite an impression on him—and on his daughter. "He just had a very powerful and yet subtle personality," said Craven. "There was some sort of charisma about him…My teenage daughter and her friend were there at the reading, and they absolutely flipped out over him."[19]

Depp got the part for the role of Glen Lantz, a teen stalked and eventually killed by Robert Englund's Freddy Krueger character. His salary was $1,200 a week for six weeks of work. "It was amazing to me," he said, "that someone wanted to pay me that much money, which was just union scale [the minimum wage for union actors]."[20]

Depp's new occupation intrigued him. "I want to keep growing and learning as much as possible," he said, "I want to fill myself in on all aspects of the industry."[21] With his music career at a standstill, he was determined to give this new endeavor a chance to succeed.

Chapter 2

The Teen Idol

Johnny Depp's acting career started out slowly. When his big break came along, it transformed him into the kind of product he desperately wanted to avoid becoming. He vowed to learn from the experience and to be true to his values with regard to future choices.

Sherilyn Fenn

Unfortunately, work as an actor cannot always be counted on, especially when just starting a career. With paying roles hard to come by, Depp accepted a part in a short student film called *Dummies*, directed by Laurie Frank. He was cast opposite a young actress by the name of Sherilyn Fenn.

The on-screen chemistry between the two was quickly apparent. It carried over off the set as well. "They really fell madly in love,"[22] said Frank. Depp and Sherilyn soon moved in together.

A Slow Start

Depp eventually got parts in two more films. The first was as co-lead with Rob Morrow in the 1985's *Private Resort*. The following year, Depp appeared with Eric Roberts and Beverly D'Angelo in *Slow Burn*. The film was made for cable television and not released in movie theaters.

Although the films did little to enhance Depp's reputation as an actor, he was not discouraged. Deep down, he still harbored hopes of resurrecting a career as a musician. Says Depp,

> I made some [bad] movies when I was first starting out but I'm not embarrassed by them, especially as I didn't think I was going to be an actor—I was just trying to make some money. I was still a musician. When I first started out, I was just given the opportunity, and there was no other way to make that kind of money. Apart from crime. I couldn't believe how much they were paying me.[23]

One day, Depp's agent told him about an offer for a role in a new movie to be directed by Oscar winner Oliver Stone. The film, *Platoon*, was about the war in Vietnam.

Platoon

The filming of *Platoon*, took place in the jungles of the Philippines. The shoot required the cast to spend fifty-four days fighting the heat, humidity, monsoon rains, and hordes of insects. Depp was cast as a GI named Lerner who acted as a translator for his platoon.

The film was a huge success and became the top-grossing movie

In the Oscar-winning movie **Platoon,** *Johnny Depp (right) played a young soldier in Vietnam. To his disappointment, however, much of his role did not make the film's final cut.*

Oliver Stone

Oliver Stone has earned a reputation as one of Hollywood's most controversial directors. His films have covered such topics as the war in Vietnam (*Platoon*, *Born on the Fourth of July*, *Heaven & Earth*), the assassination of President John F. Kennedy (*JFK*), greed in big business (*Wall Street*), President Richard Nixon (*Nixon*), 9/11 (*World Trade Center*), President George W. Bush (*W.*), and violence and mass murder (*Natural Born Killers*).

Stone has won three Academy Awards, two for directing (*Platoon*, *Born on the Fourth of July*) and one for Best Screenplay (*Midnight Express*). Films that he has directed have been nominated for a total of 31 Oscars.

of 1987. It eventually earned four Academy Awards, including Best Picture. Unfortunately, much of Depp's footage was cut in the final edits. Explained Stone, "In the scenes Lerner was in he became a focus, he was a compelling character and Depp played him as such, I ran into the problem in editing that this Lerner character ended up being more interesting than the lead character of Chris Taylor [Charlie Sheen] which would throw the scenes and effectively the entire movie out of whack if I didn't trim them down."[24]

Television Comes Calling

Depp's experience with *Platoon* disillusioned him to a degree. A band called the Rock City Angels was looking for a guitar player and Depp joined them in hopes of renewing his career as a musician.

Around this same time, Depp's agent told him that Fox TV was interested in him for a role in a new series that was in the planning stage. The show, called *Jump Street Chapel*, was about a group of young undercover cops who infiltrated high schools in an effort to identify students who were more interested in selling drugs and indulging in other illegal activities than in studying. Depp turned the part down. He did not want to commit to a possible long-term project that would monopolize his time and energy.

Spurned by Depp, Fox gave the role to an actor named Jeff Yagher. After only three weeks, however, they knew Yagher was not right as the character. They made another attempt to get Depp to reconsider his decision. Depp auditioned and immediately impressed the show's producer, Patrick Hasburgh. Some network executives, however, had reservations. Recalled Hasburgh,

> And they were all talking and one of the Fox executives would go, 'Yeah, Josh Brolin was going to be perfect for this role,' and I go, 'Josh Brolin?' I mean with all due respect, Josh is a real talented young man but did you see this other kid? You know, Depp what's-his-name? And they're going, 'You know he just looks a little bit too dangerous and a little bit too young,' and I go, 'Are you crazy? This is one of the most talented actors I've ever had the pleasure of seeing and I've only watched him work for 35 seconds.'[25]

Hasburgh stood by his convictions and Depp signed a five-year contract, with an option for a sixth year. He later recalled, "I didn't want to sign some big contract that would bind me for years…and then they called me and said, 'Would you please come in and do it?' My agents said…'The average life span of a TV series is thirteen episodes, if that. One season.' So I said O.K."[26] A salary of $45,000 per episode was hard for a struggling musician to turn down. Depp left the Rock City Angels to concentrate on the show.

Tom Hanson

In *Jump Street Chapel*, Depp was to play a young cop named Tom Hanson. Because of Hanson's youthful appearance, he is assigned to the squad of undercover cops who operate out of an abandoned chapel located on Jump Street. The idea for the show—the name was eventually changed to *21 Jump Street*—was based on a real-life police operation of a similar nature in Los Angeles.

Depp did not particularly like the character he was to play. "Hanson is not someone I'd want to have pizza with," he said. "I don't believe in having undercover cops in high school—it's spying. The only thing I have in common with Tom Hanson is that we look alike."[27]

A Star Is Born

21 Jump Street debuted on April 21, 1987. It was an immediate hit, quickly becoming the favorite show in its time slot among young females between the ages of eighteen and thirty-four.

Depp was the single most important factor in the show's suc-

Although Depp, pictured here with his 21 Jump Street castmates, experienced overnight success with the show, he was uncomfortable with his newfound teen idol status.

cess. He found his picture on the covers of magazines like *Sixteen* and *Teen Beat*. His fan mail soared and he was soon receiving ten thousand letters a week. Although most were harmless and even funny, some were of a scarier nature. Said Depp, "Kids write to me and say they are having these problems or they want to commit suicide or something. It's scary. I have to say, 'Listen, I'm just an actor, not a professional psychologist. If you need help you should go and get it.'"[28]

Depp did not enjoy the fame and adulation that came with the show's success. "Those are things that are out of my control," he said. "It's very nice to be appreciated, but I'm not really comfortable with it. I've never liked being the center of attention. It comes with the territory."[29]

Even more, Depp hated the idea of being marketed as a teen idol. He feared it would interfere with his plans for the future. As he told *Rolling Stone* in 1998, "I don't want to make a career of taking my shirt off. I'd like to shave off all my hair, even my eyebrows, try it that way. I don't fault the TV stars who do teen magazines. They took a hold of their situations, took offers that gave them the big money fast, but they were dead in two years. I don't want that."[30]

A Long-Running Hit

Depp's worst fears had been realized. He had signed a contract for a role he thought might last for, at most, a year. The show, however, was renewed. It turned into a long-term commitment that prevented him from actively pursuing movie roles that might have interested him. Said Depp, "I'd signed up for six seasons and regretted it before a single episode aired. It was the first time I could pay my rent, but I'd see all these commercials about me. I felt like a box of cereal. It was something that I had no control over. I wanted them to fire me, but they wouldn't."[31]

Because of his popularity, Depp was asked to do several public service announcements aimed at teens. Although the ideas behind the messages were praiseworthy, Depp was troubled nonetheless. In one instance, they wanted him to do a public

Johnny Depp's Tattoos

Johnny Depp has been adorning his body with tattoos since the age of seventeen. Several refer to specific people or things in his life. These include a heart tattoo with the name of his mother, Betty Sue, on his left arm; the name of his daughter, Lily-Rose, written in script above his heart; and the name of his son, Jack, on his right arm, next to a sparrow honoring the movie, *Pirates of the Caribbean*. Another tattoo on the inside of that same arm is a symbol from his movie, *The Brave*.

Perhaps Depp's most publicized tattoo is a ribbon with the words, "WINONA FOREVER," on his upper right arm. He got it when he was dating actress Winona Ryder. When the relationship ended, Depp had the "NA" removed by laser, leaving "WINO FOREVER."

Other tattoos include the head of a Cherokee Indian chief to honor his heritage, the number "3," which he considers mystical, three tiny rectangles on his right index finger, a skull and crossbones with the words, "DEATH IS CERTAIN" on his right leg, a tiny question mark over his right ankle, and three hearts representing the three members of his immediate family on his upper left arm. A more unusual tattoo—"Silence Exile Cunning" —can also be found on his arm. It is a quote from a book by James Joyce.

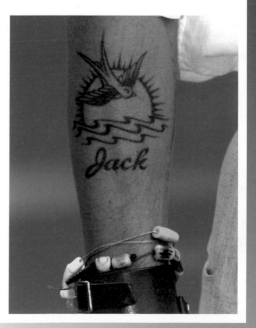

A tattoo with a reference to Jack Sparrow is shown on Johnny Depp's arm.

service announcement advising kids to stay in school. Said Depp, "I thought, well, I've been working for these people for four years. Don't they know I'm a dropout? How can I tell people to stay in school?"[32]

By the show's third season, Depp had had enough. His relationship with Sherilyn Fenn had deteriorated, and the couple broke up. Depp began dating actress Jennifer Grey, costar of the 1987 hit movie, *Dirty Dancing*. They eventually got engaged, but that relationship also did not last. Everywhere they went, they were hounded by the paparazzi. Recalled Hasburgh, "[Depp is] saying you know, 'We want to go to the store to buy some toothpaste...and two guys jump out of the bushes and start chasing us down the street. It makes no sense,' I think he wondered what was wrong with all these people ...why were these teenage girls throwing their underwear at him or waving or screaming or crying or kissing him."[33]

Depp's dissatisfaction with the show began to reveal itself in his behavior. He became disruptive on the set, doing things to try to get him fired and released from his contract. He refused to do episodes that he found objectionable, such as one in which a high school student is murdered after mistakenly being suspected of being an informer. When that did not work, he began changing lines of dialogue. He also suggested ridiculous story lines he knew had no chance of being accepted.

In an interview with television host David Letterman, Depp spoke of one particular incident that demonstrated how he felt about the show:

> I was driving down Peco, it was at 20th Century Fox and there was a massive billboard of me—of me, holding a gun with a slogan that said, 'Other kids pack lunch.' I knew right away that something had to be done about it. I thought the gun was bad news and I thought my mug up there was worse. So I commandeered a friend of mine and we went to a hardware store and bought some paint. And some brushes and rollers and all the accoutrements [accessories] and went back at about two in the morning on roller skates... and painted out the gun. And I was in the middle of turning

myself into Groucho Marx when a, you know we were very high up, when a security guard came around the corner you know, 'Halt,' that kind of thing—as they do. And we halted for a second and he looked at the billboard and he looked at me and he looked and he said, 'Well, that's you.' And I said, 'Yeah, I know.' And he said, 'Well, what are you doing?' and I said, 'Well, I don't like it, you know. I think it's wrong.' So he sorta looked frustrated and he looked at his watch and said, 'All right, just hurry.' Never heard about it again. The billboard was gone in fact.[34]

The Bad Boy

Depp's behavior became more erratic offscreen as well. One incident in March of 1989 made front-page headlines in the tabloids. Depp was visiting with friends at a Vancouver hotel where he had stayed on occasion. A security guard refused to let him in, leading to a shoving incident between the two. The police were summoned and Depp was arrested for assault and mischief. He was detained in the Vancouver central police station overnight.

Depp accepted full responsibility for his actions and the charges were dropped. Said his attorney, Richard Israels, "The learned trial judge granted him an absolute discharge. That's the most lenient disposition [ruling] available to the Court and it means that Depp is deemed in law not to be convicted of the offense. Therefore he has no criminal record."[35]

The run-in with the law added to Depp's image as a hothead and rebel. Hasburgh looked at it differently. "It was the press descending on this kid for another headline," he said, "trying to turn him into...this rebel without a cause."[36]

Winona Ryder

A couple months after his arrest in Vancouver, Depp attended the New York premiere of the movie *Great Balls of Fire*. While there, he noticed the 17-year-old costar of the film, Winona

Johnny Depp first saw Winona Ryder at the New York premier for Great Balls of Fire, *although they did not actually meet for several months after.*

Ryder. They were not formally introduced until several months later at the Chateau Marmont in West Hollywood. There was an instant attraction between them. Remembered Ryder, "I thought he might be one of those TV star Hollywood jerks—but he wasn't, he was really, really shy....We fell in love that night even though we probably didn't know it."[37]

The young couple began spending all their free time together. When *21 Jump Street* started production on its fourth season, Ryder visited Depp on the set whenever she had the chance. That September, she began work on the movie *Mermaids* in Boston. Distance could not keep them apart, however. Said Hasburgh, "He was a guy who was working his [behind] off, and he would fly to the east coast to meet his girlfriend, have dinner and fly back."[38]

The following January, Depp and Ryder got engaged. As a way of declaring his love to the world, he got a tattoo stating "Winona Forever" on his right arm.

John Waters

While Depp was courting Ryder, he began getting offers to do films. Despite his dissatisfaction with *21 Jump Street*, he still fulfilled his contractual obligations. Said the show's co-creator and co-executive producer Stephen J. Cannell, "He goes, 'I really, really, really hope we get cancelled, because I do have a lot of good film offers and I want to move on. But I want you to know that I signed a contract with you, and that if we get renewed I will be there.' And I just thought that was so standup of him…to do that. And, as it turned out, we got cancelled so he got his wish."[39]

Most of the offers Depp received were for roles similar to that of his Tom Hanson character. One that was not was from eccentric filmmaker John Waters. Waters had gained a measure of notoriety through his movies *Pink Flamingos*, *Polyester*, and *Hairspray*. His new film, *Cry-Baby*, was to be a rock 'n' roll musical satire of the

John Waters offered Depp the first of many quirky roles, that of Wade "Cry Baby" Walker, in Waters' film, Cry Baby.

teen movies of the early 1950s.

For the lead characters, Waters wanted actors "who can take a step back and laugh at themselves good-naturedly."[40] After doing some research, he decided that Depp was the one he wanted for the lead part, a teenage delinquent named Wade "Cry-Baby" Walker. Said Waters, "When Johnny told me how much he hated the teen-idol image, I told him to stick with us—we'll kill that, we'll get rid of that in a second, because we're going to make fun of your teen-idol status from first frame to last."[41]

Depp enjoyed working with Waters on *Cry-Baby*. He said, "[Waters would] listen to ideas about adding or taking out lines. If I was having a problem with something he'd rehearse with me."[42] Since his character was a teenage musician, Depp also enjoyed being able to use his musical background to help the film's musical supervisors decide on the gear to be used in the band numbers.

The script was exactly what Depp was looking for:

Cry-Baby came along at a good time for me. "I had been looking at film ideas for a while and was getting disillusioned. Most of what I read was flat, just schlock. I was sent so many scripts which just echoed what I was doing on *Jump Street*, and I wanted something that would be totally different. John first sent me a letter and then we talked a bit and met, and then he gave me a script. I was so excited because not only was it really funny, but it made fun of all those clichés and sensitive hero roles I had been reading for so long.[43]

It was the type of quirky role for which he would become known.

Chapter 3

Ups and Downs

The trappings of fame are not all positive. Johnny Depp had his first major success in a film directed by Tim Burton, and he found that the life of a celebrity in the public eye could have as many drawbacks as it has benefits.

Edward Scissorhands

As a child, Tim Burton had difficulty expressing himself and communicating with others. He often felt he did not fit in. As an adult, he expressed those feelings of isolation in his script for *Edward Scissorhands*. Edward is a young man with scissor blades for hands. Said Burton,

> The idea actually came from a drawing I did a long time ago. It…was linked to a character who wants to touch but can't, who was both creative and destructive….The manifestation of the image…probably came to the surface when I was a teenager, because it is a very teenage thing. It had to do with relationships. I just felt I couldn't communicate.[44]

When Depp read the script, he knew the role was perfect for him. Now he had to convince the director. Said Burton:

> I'd seen his television show [*21 Jump Street*] but that's all I knew about him. Then I met him and he reminded me of

Originally, the studio had bigger stars in mind for the role of Edward Scissorhands, but when director Tim Burton met Depp in his audition, Burton insisted on Depp for the lead role.

the old star type that gives you a special feeling....He's one of those people who comes across as both old and young. He's a great character actor in many ways...a leading man. That's what struck me about him from the very beginning.[45]

The studio had bigger names in mind for the role: Tom Hanks, Tom Cruise, William Hurt, Robert Downey Jr. After meeting with Depp, however, Burton made his decision. He simply told him, "You are Edward Scissorhands."[46]

The filming was enjoyable for Depp for another, more personal reason. Winona Ryder had been scheduled to appear in *The Godfather: Part III*, which was being filmed in Italy. Shortly after arriving in Rome, however, she fell ill with an upper respiratory infection and had to drop out of the film. This freed her for the role of Depp's love interest in *Edward Scissorhands*.

Burton had no fears about Depp and Ryder working together:

I don't think their relationship affected the movie in a negative way. Perhaps it might have if it had been a different kind of a movie, something that was tapping more into some positive or negative side of their relationship. But this was such a fantasy...they were very professional and didn't bring any weird stuff to the set.[47]

Depp's touching performance in *Edward Scissorhands* was the biggest factor in the film's success. Most critics praised his work, and he received a Golden Globe nomination for Best Actor in a Musical or Comedy. He followed up his success with a part in the sequel to *A Nightmare on Elm Street* called *Freddy's Dead: The Final Nightmare* and the role of Inuit hunter Axel Blackmar in Emir Kusturica's *Arizona Dream*.

Unfortunately, Depp's relationship with Ryder had begun to suffer. Their film careers kept them apart a good bit of the time. When they were together, paparazzi and reporters eager to intrude on their private moments hounded them. Said Ryder,

I had never really had a boyfriend before and I was going through lots of wonderfully positive emotional growth with

Johnny, but the hordes of paparazzi and writers trailing us around all the time really took a toll on our relationship... You are trying to figure out your own feelings and interpret them as they are very powerful feelings—then some writer comes along who doesn't even know us and is writing all about how our relationship is.[48]

Benny and Joon

Depp's next role was in director Jeremiah Chechik's romantic comedy, *Benny and Joon.* He played the part of an eccentric young man who falls in love with an emotionally disturbed young woman, played by Mary Stuart Masterson. Depp's character is a big fan of silent movies (movies from the early 1900s that were without sound) and silent movie stars such as Buster Keaton. In real life, Depp was also a fan. The role gave him a chance to reenact slapstick routines in the style of Keaton and Charlie Chaplin. He recalled, "I had such a great time rediscovering Keaton, Chaplin and Harold Lloyd. Comedy, especially when it is so physical, is extremely demanding. I developed an even greater respect for those guys as I began to try to do what they had accomplished in such a seemingly effortless way."[49]

Depp's work was well received by the critics. "Mr. Depp may look nothing like Buster Keaton," wrote Janet Maslin of *The New York Times*, "but there are times when he genuinely seems to become the Great Stone Face, bringing Keaton's mannerisms sweetly and magically to life."[50] His touching performance earned him a second Golden Globe nomination.

What's Eating Gilbert Grape?

Depp and Ryder split up and went their separate ways in June of 1993. "I remember us desperately hating being hounded," said Ryder. "It was horrible and it definitely took its toll on our relationship. Every day we heard that we were either cheating on each other or that we were broken up when we weren't. It was

Buster Keaton

Together with Charlie Chaplin and Harold Lloyd, Buster Keaton is generally considered one of the three great comedy actors of the silent film era. He developed his physical style of comedy while performing in his family's vaudeville act, known as "The Three Keatons." As part of the act, his father threw young Buster around the stage. He was billed as, "The Little Boy Who Can't Be Damaged."

In the 1920s, Keaton became a major player in Hollywood, writing, directing and starring in a series of films, with his greatest work usually considered to be *The General* (1926). Keaton's movie character is best known for his physical comedy. His trademark deadpan expression earned him the nickname, "The Great Stone Face."

Keaton's career took a downturn when talking films came along. He made a comeback of sorts in the late 1930s. Through the 1940s, 1950s and 1960s, he had parts in several feature films, and also appeared many times on television. He died at the age of 70 in 1966.

Buster Keaton's nickname was "The Great Stone Face."

Even though Depp had just broken up with actress Winona Ryder, he gave a memorable performance as Gilbert in What's Eating Gilbert Grape.

like this constant mosquito buzzing around us."[51]

Depp tried his best to throw himself into his work. His next role was as the title character in *What's Eating Gilbert Grape?* His characterizations in previous films made him Swedish director Lasse Hallstrom's ideal choice for the part. "Gilbert is very much an observer, a reactor on the move," said Hallstrom. "Johnny Depp was the perfect actor He has the sensitivity that Gilbert Grape needs."[52]

In the film, Depp played a young man who becomes responsible for the care of his family after his father abandons them. He gave another impressive performance despite his depression following the breakup with Ryder. Costar Leonardo DiCaprio remembers,

> He was *extremely* like Gilbert. But it wasn't something Johnny was trying to do. It naturally came out of him. I never quite understood what he was going through, because it wasn't

some *big emotional drama* that was happening every day on the set—but subtle things I'd see in him would make me question what was going on. There's an element of Johnny that's extremely nice and extremely cool, but at the same time, he's hard to figure out. But that's what makes him interesting.[53]

Depp later said his personal problems might have helped him better understand the character of Gilbert. "It was a hard time for me," he said. "I was just having a weird time myself, personally, which kind of helped me creatively…I don't know if I subconsciously made myself miserable for a little bit because I knew that's what the character needed, or if it was just what I had to deal with at that particular time. I was drinking a lot. I poisoned myself regularly."[54]

With his life at a low point, Depp had a scare that made him rethink his priorities. As he described it,

"I was sitting around having drinks with a couple of friends around this time and suddenly my heart started racing to 200 beats per minute. I couldn't get it to stop and my panic was rising—finally I ended up in an emergency room getting some kind of shot that stopped my heart so it could be restarted at its proper rhythm. That scared…me as I assume it would just about anyone—I started thinking differently about things."[55]

The Viper Room

Depp enlisted the help of his older sister, Christie, as his personal manager. He decided to invest some of his earnings. An opportunity presented itself to buy into a nightclub on Sunset Boulevard. The location had originally been the site of The Melody Room, a club owned by gangster Bugsy Siegel in the 1940s. In 1993, it was called The Central, owned by Anthony Fox. Depp and a friend, musician Chuck E. Weiss, invested $350,000 to obtain

Johnny Depp invested in the Viper Room as a place for he and his friends to hang out and listen to music. In 1993, however, it became known as the club where actor (and friend of Depp's) River Phoenix died from an overdose of drugs.

51% ownership of the club from Fox. It had long been a dream of Depp's to own a small club where he and his friends could hang out, listening to the music they loved. Said Depp, "I thought maybe I could turn this into a 1930s be-bop speak-easy with viper music—Fats Waller and Cab Calloway— good music which nobody else is playing."[56]

The Viper Room opened on August 14, 1993. The opening night was a benefit for the Starlight Foundation, an association that helps children diagnosed with serious illnesses. Tom Petty and The Heartbreakers were among the acts that night. Also attending the festivities were Depp's *Benny and Joon* costar Mary Stuart Masterson, Crispin Glover, Rebecca De Mornay, Quentin Tarantino, Christina Applegate, Julianne Phillips, Patricia Arquette, and Tim Burton, Depp's director from *Edward Scissorhands*. Opening night was a hit, and $14,000 was raised for the foundation.

Tragedy

The Viper Room received positive reviews and quickly became one of Hollywood's "in" spots. It was a place where Depp could relax and jam together with his musician friends.

On the night of October 30, 1993, actor River Phoenix was in attendance, together with his brother Joaquin, his girlfriend Samantha Mathis, and Michael Balzary, better known as Flea, from the Red Hot Chili Peppers. River brought his guitar along with him, intending to perform later that evening. Unfortunately, he never got the chance.

As the evening progressed, River became incoherent, clearly under the influence of some combination of alcohol or drugs. Shortly after midnight, he made a visit to the washroom where he likely ingested a combination of cocaine and heroin. He became violently ill and stumbled outside to the sidewalk in front of the club. When he began going into convulsions, his brother called 9-1-1 for an ambulance. River died in the ambulance en route to a local hospital.

The media immediately played up the incident, hinting that the club was a refuge for drug users. The accusations infuriated Depp. "They made it a fiasco of lies to sell magazines," he said. "They said he was doing drugs in my club, that I allow people to do drugs in my club. What a ridiculous thought!"[57]

Ed Wood

Shortly before the River Phoenix tragedy, Depp had taken on his next role. It was another unusual character, but this time it was a real person. He was selected by Tim Burton to play the role of Ed Wood, dubbed by many as the "World's Worst Film Director." Wood was the driving force behind films such as *Glen or Glenda* and *Plan Nine from Outer Space,* considered among the worst movies ever made. Among other things, Wood's films were known for unusual casting, poor special effects, and tiny budgets. *Plan Nine*, for example, starred horror actor Bela Lugosi, former pro wrestler Tor Johnson, TV horror hostess Vampira, and the

River Phoenix and Johnny Depp

Actor River Phoenix was just twenty-three years old when he died of a drug overdose outside Johnny Depp's Viper Room in West Hollywood. In honor of his friend, Depp closed the club for a week following Phoenix's death on October 31, 1993. He continued to close The Viper Room on that date every year thereafter, until he sold his share in the club in 2004.

There were several parallels between the careers of the two young men. Both Depp and Phoenix shared a passion for music. Each began playing the guitar at a young age. Both moved to Los Angeles from their homes in Florida in order to further their careers. Depp left Miramar together with his wife Lori and his bandmates with The Kids. Phoenix's family left Winter Haven so that he and his sister could follow their dreams of becoming recording artists.

Both Depp and Phoenix had a degree of success in television. While Depp starred in *21 Jump Street*, Phoenix had a role in the short-lived series, *Seven Brides for Seven Brothers*. Both would later be nominated for Academy Awards for their work on the silver screen.

psychic Criswell. Lugosi died during the filming and was replaced by Wood's chiropractor, who played all his scenes holding his cape in front of his face. Props included plastic toy flying saucers that can be seen supported by visible strings.

Wood's personal life made him a fascinating character for Depp to portray. A Marine who was a decorated World War II hero, Wood was also a transvestite—he liked to wear women's clothing. Depp threw himself into the role. "There is something fun and sort of exciting about doing something that shocks people," he said, "and (a male) wearing women's clothing makes people really uncomfortable."[58]

Depp's performance in the film won over both fans and critics alike. For the third time, he was nominated for a Golden Globe

Award for Best Actor in a Comedy or Musical. Hugh Grant won, however, for his role in *Four Weddings and a Funeral*.

Kate Moss

After the filming of *Ed Wood* was completed, Depp happened to meet British supermodel Kate Moss at a New York restaurant. There was an immediate connection between the two, even though Depp, at age thirty, was ten years older than Kate.

In the past, Depp had tried to be honest with the media about matters in his personal life. "It's very hard to have a personal life in this town," said Depp. "My relationship with Winona, it was my mistake to be as open as we were, but I thought if we were honest it would destroy that curiosity monster. Instead it fed it, gave people license to feel they were part of it."[59] With this in mind, he tried to keep his relationship with Kate out of the limelight. Unfortunately, it was practically impossible to do so. Rumors circulated that the pair either were—or would soon be—engaged. Another run-in with the law added to the media frenzy.

The Mark Hotel

On the night of September 12, 1994, Depp and Kate were in their room at New York's Mark Hotel. The night security guard received a call to investigate a disturbance in the room at about 5:00 the next morning. When he arrived there, he found several smashed items of furniture. The guard told Depp that he would have to leave. Depp offered to pay for any damages, but the guard was insistent. The police were called in and Depp was arrested on two counts of criminal mischief.

Although his lawyer hinted that the charges for the damage were overblown, Depp did not deny his involvement. As he explained the incident,

> Very simply, I had a bad day. I'd been chased by paparazzi and was feeling a bit like Novelty Boy…I lost it. It was the

Johnny Depp is escorted out of the 19th Precinct in New York following his arrest on September 13, 1994. Depp was accused of damaging furnishings in his room at the Mark Hotel.

culmination of many things, a bad spark, and I went off. I did what I felt was necessary. Thank God it wasn't a human being but a hotel room that I took it out on… I did my business, and they came up to the room. By that point I had cooled down. I said, 'I'll of course pay for any damages. I apologize.' That wasn't enough…The next thing you know, the police were at the door.[60]

Depp eventually paid for the damages, and the judge dismissed the charges. "I thought it was funny," he would later say. "I have to go to jail for assaulting a picture frame or a lamp!... I have a lot of love inside me and a lot of anger inside as well. If I love somebody, then I'm gonna love 'em. If I'm angry and I've got to lash out or hit somebody, I'm going to do it and I don't care what the repercussions are. Anger doesn't pay rent, it's gotta go. It's gotta be evicted."[61]

After this incident, Depp focused on channeling his energies into his work. The result was a series of unusual roles that helped solidify his growing reputation as an actor.

Chapter 4

Oddballs, Eccentrics, and Outcasts

Johnny Depp's vision of his future in the industry did not include leading man roles in top-grossing films. Instead, the roles that interested him were those that pushed the envelope, quirky characters that other actors might try to avoid. "I decided early on to be patient and wait for the roles that interested me," he said, "not the roles that would advance my career. I never wanted to be remembered for being a star."[62]

A New Friend

Following his success in *Ed Wood*, Depp was offered the lead in the romantic comedy, *Don Juan DeMarco*. The movie is the story of a young man who believes himself to be Don Juan, the world's greatest lover. He becomes the patient of a psychiatrist who takes on his case despite being on the verge of retirement.

After reading the script, Depp thought the part of the psychiatrist would be perfect for legendary actor Marlon Brando, one of his idols. Before he accepted the role, Depp had one request. "Johnny said he'd only do the film," recalled writer-director Jeremy Leven, "if Brando played the psychiatrist. At that point I thought the project was dead in the water, only to receive a second shock, hearing that Marlon was also interested."[63]

Johnny Depp played the lead in Don Juan DeMarco, *opposite Marlon Brando. Depp accepted the role on the condition that Brando played the psychiatrist.*

The pairing of the two actors was a dream come true for Depp. It was also very symbolic. Brando was generally acknowledged to be the greatest actor of his generation. Many considered Depp as Brando's successor to that title. Working together on the film, the pair developed a close friendship and respect for each other. Said actress Faye Dunaway, their costar in the film, "Marlon adored Johnny—he loved his genuineness and his modesty. Marlon could spot a fake a mile away, which is why he instantly knew Johnny was the real thing."[64]

The combination of Depp and Brando was a main attraction of the film, and Depp again received good reviews. Said Barbara Shulgasser of the *San Francisco Chronicle*, "Depp keeps proving with each new film that he can do anything."[65] However, it was not one of Brando's best efforts. Wrote Roger Ebert, "Actors often talk about how they'd like to work with Brando. [Depp] could teach him some things."[66]

James Dean

Johnny Depp is one of several young actors who at one time or another have been characterized as "the next James Dean." Dean became a cultural icon whose popularity was based on roles in three major motion pictures: *East of Eden* (1955), *Rebel Without a Cause* (1955), and *Giant* (1956). He embodied the spirit of the disaffected youth of the day. His characters were misunderstood outcasts who felt such anxieties as feelings of being misunderstood by parents and other adults.

Dean's brief cinematic career was cut short when he was killed in an automobile accident in 1955 at the age of 24. He is the only actor to receive two posthumous nominations for Academy Awards, the first for his 1955 role of Cal Trask in *East of Eden* and the second a year later for his role of Jett Rink in *Giant*.

In Search of a Blockbuster

Depp followed his success in *Don Juan DeMarco* with another quirky role in Jim Jarmusch's Western, *Dead Man*. He played the part of William Blake, an accountant who travels out west and becomes a hunted outlaw in the late 1800s. The film is a slow-moving western, filmed in black and white, with an eerie musical score by rocker Neil Young.

Dead Man was met with mixed reviews. Many believed it was time for Depp to give up his penchant for only taking oddball parts. Critics and fans alike wanted him to take the next step and move on to more mainstream, blockbuster-type movies. Even Depp hinted it was time for a change, saying, "I hope this is the last of these innocents I play."[67]

He still, however, held out for roles that interested him. Said his agent, Tracey Jacobs, "Do I want him to be in a movie that does $400 million? Of course!... Let me make this really clear... *he* wants to be in a commercial movie. It just has to be the right timing and the right one, that's all. Hopefully he'll be available when those come along again."[68]

Some critics, however, viewed Depp's next role as his first to be accepted for purely commercial reasons. The movie was *Nick of Time*, an update of an Alfred Hitchcock thriller. Depp played the part of an accountant forced to carry out a political assassination in order to save the life of his young daughter. "When I read *Nick of Time*," said Depp, "I could see the guy mowing the grass, watering his lawn...and I liked the challenge of playing him. He's

Jack Kerouac and the Beat Generation

When Johnny Depp was a young man, he became entranced by the work of Jack Kerouac, who was a legendary literary figure remembered as being one of the pioneers of what he termed the Beat Generation. The name originally came from the phrase "beaten down," meaning tired.

Fundamentals promoted by the Beat Generation writers included free expression, the questioning of authority, rejection of materialism, experimentation with drugs, an interest in Eastern religions, and alternative forms of sexuality, particularly homosexuality. Other founding members of the group included Allen Ginsberg, William S. Burroughs, and Herbert Huncke.

Kerouac's most influential work was his novel, *On the Road*, published in 1957. It became an immediate sensation and helped earn him the nickname, "King of the Beats." The Beat Generation of the 1950s eventually spawned the hippie movement of the 1960s. A significant difference between the two movements was the hippie concern with civil rights and antiwar themes. The beats were less politically oriented.

nothing like me…it gives me a chance to play a straight, normal, suit-and-tie guy."[69]

Unfortunately, the movie did not approach expectations at the box office. "It's a competent film," wrote Edward Guthmann, "but…it ends on a flat note and strains credibility too often."[70] Another critic was not as kind, saying, "You don't do a movie that crappy unless you think it's going to make a ton of coin."[71] Depp's next two movies were scheduled to be *Divine Rapture*, a black comedy, and *The Cull*, a political thriller. Both films were delayed, and then eventually cancelled, because of financial problems. The search for a commercial success continued.

Settling Down?

Depp had purchased a mansion in Los Angeles in October 1995. It was supposedly the former home of silent film star Bela Lugosi. After years of living out of hotel rooms, he finally had a place to call home. Said Depp, "I just loved the house; it's such a strange design, very unusual architecture. It is like a weird little castle in the middle of Hollywood, but I'm hardly ever there."[72]

The purchase of the house spurred rumors that Depp was planning to settle down. The tabloids reported that he and Kate

In October 1995, Johnny Depp bought the former home of silent film star Bela Lugosi.

were either engaged, planning on getting married—or splitting up. Depp ignored the rumors and prepared for his next role.

A Critical Success

Depp's next project was *Donnie Brasco*. It resulted in another outstanding performance. The movie was based on the real life story of FBI agent Joe Pistone, who infiltrated the New York City mob. One of the attractions of the role for Depp was the opportunity to work with Al Pacino. "Working with Pacino," he said, "was one of the great learning experiences of my entire career. I stuck by him and watched him and absorbed his technique. He is a great actor, one of the truly great actors ever—how could I not learn from him?"[73]

The Depp-Pacino combination proved to be a winning one. *Donnie Brasco* was one of the most critically acclaimed films of the year.

Johnny Depp, Director

Depp had long dreamed of directing a movie. In past years, he had directed a short film but never a full-length work. He finally got the opportunity to do so in late 1996. Together with his brother, Dan, Depp adapted a screenplay of a Gregory McDonald novel called, *Raphael: Final Days*. It would become *The Brave*, the story of a Native American man who agrees to be killed on film in exchange for $50,000.

In addition to writing and directing the film, Depp also played the part of Raphael, the Native American. Marlon Brando agreed to play the part of the fictional film's producer. "Marlon coming and doing this film with me was an incredible blessing," said Depp. "It was beyond a dream."[74]

The experience of directing was much more difficult than Depp had anticipated. "It was the hardest thing that I have ever done," he said. "I had no idea that it was so complicated...I am glad I did it and am very proud of the results but I am in no hurry to

In addition to starring in the film **The Brave**, *Johnny Depp also wrote the screenplay and directed it.*

repeat the experience."[75]

The Brave debuted at the Cannes International Film Festival in May 1997. It was poorly received by the critics and never released for audiences in the United States. In his book, *My Year of Flops*, Nathan Rabin described it as "a morbid, maudlin [overly sentimental] oddity that starts off slowly and never finds its footing. Having suffered through Depp's well-meaning but dreary directorial debut, I can assure you that American audiences deprived of a legal means of checking out *The Brave* really aren't missing much."[76]

The negative reaction, however, did not discourage Depp. "Will I direct again?" he said. "Yes, definitely. I don't think that I would direct again and be in it, or be the lead role in it. But…I'll definitely do it again."[77]

Another Breakup

While dealing with this disappointment, Depp was also facing troubles in his personal life. It appeared that although he might be ready to finally settle down, Kate had other plans, preferring to maintain her globetrotting lifestyle. The issue that finally caused their breakup was Depp's interest in becoming a father and starting a family. "The time was obviously right for me," he said, "and I started to talk about it with Kate. I thought she would react really enthusiastic, but she didn't. Kate immediately said that children weren't an option at the moment. That came as a shock to me. I was already getting happy about it and I never considered the fact that she might not be ready for it."[78]

Depp, however, refused to blame Kate for the breakup. "It's my own fault Kate left me," he said. "I can be a real pain in the butt and act really irritating. Especially when I'm working on a movie and it isn't going the way it is supposed to be. It gets on my nerves and I get annoying."[79] Despite the breakup, Depp and Kate continued to remain good friends.

Another Film, Another Idol

Once again, Depp threw himself into his work. He followed his directorial debut with the lead role in *Fear and Loathing in Las Vegas*, based on the book by Hunter S. Thompson, who was the originator of gonzo journalism in which the reporter is part of the story itself. Because of this, the line between fiction and

Co-stars Benicio Del Toro, left, and Johnny Depp, right, join Hunter Thompson, center, author of the classic pop culture novel Fear and Loathing in Las Vegas, *at the premier of the film adaptation of Thompson's book.*

nonfiction is blurred.

The book that the movie was based on was one of Depp's all-time favorites. "I remember reading it at seventeen," he said, "and cackling like a banshee. I loved it! I went on to read the majority of Hunter's writing. When the idea came to do it as a film, I jumped at the chance."[80]

Thompson allowed Depp to stay with him in his Colorado home in order to get to know him better. The two became close friends. "Hunter is indelible [unforgettable]," said Depp. "He is like a disease you've got. He slips under your skin, takes root into your blood and your pores...He haunts you."[81] The preparation for—and filming of—*Fear and Loathing in Las Vegas* was an exhausting experience for Depp. When it was over, he felt he had done justice to the book and to Thompson. The critics disagreed. The movie was panned in most quarters. Roger Ebert of the *Chicago Sun-Times* called it "a horrible mess of a movie without shape, trajectory or purpose."[82]

Stuff

In 1992, Johnny Depp directed a 12-minute film with Gibby Haynes, a fellow musician. Filmed at the home of John Frusciante, former guitarist with the Red Hot Chili Peppers, it was called *Stuff*.

After quitting the Peppers in 1992, Frusciante became a recluse and fell victim to drug addiction and depression. *Stuff* depicts the chaos into which his life had descended. Frusciante was preoccupied with painting. The walls of his house were covered with odd graffiti. Painting equipment, guitars, and empty bottles were scattered everywhere. Timothy Leary, 1960s drug guru and godfather of Depp's former girlfriend Winona Ryder, also appears in the film.

A Musical Interlude

Disappointed by the response to the film, Depp decided to take a break from making movies. He headed to Mustique, a private island in the West Indies, for a brief vacation. The band Oasis happened to be there at the same time, recording their latest album, *Be Here Now*.

Depp was sitting in with them at the studio one day when guitar player Noel Gallagher became unable to continue recording. Depp filled in for him and performed admirably. Gallagher later said, "I'll tell you just how good Depp is—when it came time to tour in support of the album I tried to duplicate the slide riff he put on the track—I couldn't do it. It took me about six months of trying to actually finally be good enough with it to actually play it live."[83]

Depp also contributed to several documentaries during this period. One of them—*The Source*—was about the Beat generation writers of the 1950s. In it, he had the chance to play his old hero, Jack Kerouac.

By late 1998, Depp was anxious to get back to work in front of the cameras. In *The Astronaut's Wife*, he played an astronaut who has been touched by an alien force during a mission in space. The film was not considered one of his better efforts. "The almost-always-superb Depp is the weakest acting link," wrote Dustin Putman. "Regardless of the palpable air of menace he presents here, his character is a one-dimensional villain, and every facial expression he vents off practically screams, 'I'm the baddie here!'"[84]

As soon as he finished filming, Depp packed his bags and headed off to France for his next project. The trip would be fruitful for both his career and his personal life.

The Ninth Gate

Depp's next role was in director Roman Polanski's film, *The Ninth Gate*. Polanski is a controversial figure in the movie industry. He was born in Paris, France, but grew up in Poland. When

Germany invaded Poland, Polanski managed to avoid persecution by the Nazis. He eventually made his way to the United States and became a respected filmmaker whose hits included *Rosemary's Baby* and *Chinatown*. His life was touched by tragedy in 1969 when his wife, actress Sharon Tate, was slain in the infamous Manson family murders. Polanski eventually returned to Europe in 1978 to avoid prosecution on a charge of having sex with an underage girl. He continued to make films, and won an Oscar in 2003 for *The Pianist*.

Polanski's reputation as a director is what attracted Depp, rather than the screenplay for the film. "I think Polanski is one of the few filmmakers who nearly did a perfect film, a couple of them," he said. "*Chinatown* was almost perfect. It may be perfect. And I was really excited about the prospect of going to work with him."[85]

The complex story centers on a book dealer (Depp) who is hired to find copies of a book—*The Nine Gates Of The Kingdom Of Shadows*—supposedly written, in part, by Satan himself. Others who also want the books pursue him. Those who come in contact with the books suffer strange deaths.

Many were disappointed in the film. Wrote James Berardinelli, "Polanski has not done anything worthwhile in the last two decades, and *The Ninth Gate* will not raise his name back into the public's consciousness."[86] Despite the negative reviews, Depp was lauded for his work. "By lending his acting magic to *The Ninth Gate*," wrote Betty Jo Tucker, "Depp makes director Roman Polanski's sometimes plodding new thriller worth watching."[87]

Vanessa Paradis

One of the actresses who auditioned for a part in the movie was a young woman named Vanessa Paradis. Vanessa was a singer and model as well as an actress. She had exploded on the scene with a hit pop single, "Joe Le Taxi," back in 1987 at the age of fourteen. Since then, she had recorded several albums and won the French equivalent of an Oscar—a César Award—for Most Promising Actress for her role in *Noce Blanche*.

Johnny Depp attends the 63rd Annual Golden Globes with girlfriend Vanessa Paradis.

One evening during the filming of *The Ninth Gate*, Depp was having dinner at the Hotel Costes with director Polanski and a few members of the crew. Depp had met Vanessa several years before, and on this night he noticed Vanessa at the bar and invited her to his table. As Vanessa's biographer, Alain Grasset, described it, "They were exchanging secret glances. When he invited her to his table, he made a place for her to sit down and she said she went straight for it."[88]

Hours later, the couple was still busy talking. Vanessa's effect on Depp was explosive:

I pretty much fell in love with Vanessa the moment I set eyes on her. As a person, I was pretty much a lost cause at that point of my life. She turned all that around for me with her incredible tenderness and understanding. Very quickly, I realized I couldn't live without her. She made me feel like a real human being instead of someone Hollywood had manufactured. It sounds incredibly corny and phony, but that's exactly what happened to me and what she has meant to me.[89]

Depp and Vanessa began seeing each other every day. He eventually rented an apartment in Montmartre, Paris, in order to be closer to her. Less than three months later, Vanessa was pregnant.

Chapter 5

The Family Man

Depp's life would never be the same after the birth of his children. He embraced the role of father and family man. Having children also made him reconsider the direction in which his film career was heading.

During her pregnancy, Depp and Vanessa moved into her parents' house outside Paris. Depp appreciated the atmosphere of the city, away from the prying eyes that followed him everywhere he went in the States. He enjoyed all the attractions Paris had to offer, from its restaurants to its museums.

Depp's feelings toward the city were reciprocated in turn by the French people. In April 1999, he was awarded an honorary César Award (the national film award of France) for his work in the field of cinema. Depp was both honored and surprised. "That was a weird little deal," he said. "I was really taken aback by that: It was the kind of thing you get just before you die, like a lifetime achievement award…I was really touched, because I'm not big on awards."[90]

Temper, Temper

There were still occasions, however, when Depp's hostility toward the media got the best of him. One of these was in January 1999, while he was in England to film Tim Burton's *Sleepy Hollow*.

Depp was out for a special dinner with Vanessa and several

Johnny Depp smiles at the standing ovation after he receives an honorary César during the annual César awards ceremony in Paris.

friends at the Mirabelle restaurant in London. The paparazzi descended on the restaurant and refused to let Depp and his group enjoy their evening. "I went out and talked to them," he said. "I said, 'Look, guys, I know what you're after. I understand you have a job to do. But you're just not going to turn this into a circus. Just give us a break. You're not going to get what you want tonight. I'll see you another time."[91] The paparazzi, however, would not leave.

Depp picked up a stick that was resting against a door, and swung at the first photographer. The confrontation resulted in Depp being taken into custody for disturbing the peace. He was released several hours later. Because of incidents such as this, Depp came to appreciate the French attitude toward celebrity. As he said, "Here no one is interested in me. It doesn't matter that my name is Johnny Depp and that I do something in the movie business."[92]

A Reason for Living

Five months after the episode in London, Lily-Rose Melody Depp was born. Depp and Vanessa both liked the name Lily. Her mother suggested the name Rose. They combined the two names, and then added Melody from the Serge Gainsbourg song, "The Ballad of Melody Nelson."

Depp's life was totally altered. As he later described it, "I just kind of stumbled around for 35 years, and then when my daughter arrived, it was like 'Now, I see.' Suddenly everything else is just kind of shavings, morsels, little tidbits. And this is what it's all about. This is real life. Boy, it couldn't have come at a better time."[93]

Becoming a father made Depp even more leery of the paparazzi:

> I had an incident with a really dumb magazine called *Voici*, where they printed a photograph of Lily-Rose, a long-lens shot from very far away, and I just went ballistic...I just wanted to beat whoever was responsible into the earth—I just wanted to rip him apart. They can do anything they want to me...but not my kid, not my pure, innocent little baby. She didn't ask to be in this circus.[94]

Walking the Walk

While Depp was adjusting to his new role as a parent, *Sleepy Hollow* was released to generally glowing reviews. Depp's performance was praised by *Rolling Stone*, which said he was "at his heartfelt and hilarious best."[95] The magazine was not alone in its praise. The film won several awards, as did Depp. These included a Blockbuster Entertainment Award for Favorite Actor in a Horror Film.

One form of recognition that Depp never expected to receive, but was awarded in 1999, was a star on the Hollywood Walk of Fame. Despite having had his battles with the town that is the center of the movie industry, he was still touched. "I have

Johnny Depp walks on his "star" on the Hollywood Walk of Fame.

to admit that I was kind of honored," he said, "in the sense that that is one of the old Hollywood traditions…it was sort of touching, in a way. The strongest image that stuck in my head was the fact that my daughter… in 40 years or 60 years or 70 years, she can walk down that street and say, oh yeah, there's my Pop's star. There's something kind of nice about it as well. But, yeah, initially I was a little astounded by the offer."[96]

A Change in Direction

Depp took his role as a father very seriously. He began to change his personal habits, cutting down on his drinking and smoking. He was totally devoted to Lily-Rose. Said Depp,

> This baby has given me life. I worked before, sure, I lived, but mostly I just existed. I see this amazing, beautiful pure angel thing wake up in the morning and smile, and nothing can touch that. She gives me the opportunity to experience something new every day. And to love, so deeply. She is the *only* reason to wake up in the morning, the only reason to take a breath.[97]

Depp began planning his next career moves with his daughter in mind. He made several appearances on London television, and accepted cameo roles in several low-budget films. By doing this, he was able to limit time spent in the U.S., away from his family. His films in this period included *Before Night Falls*, *The Man*

The Hollywood Walk of Fame

There is a stretch of sidewalk in Hollywood that is recognized around the world. Known as the "Hollywood Walk of Fame," it runs for eighteen blocks along both sides of Hollywood Boulevard from Gower Avenue to La Brea Avenue and both sides of Vine Street from Yucca Street to Sunset Boulevard. It exists as a monument to the personalities who helped make Hollywood the entertainment capital of the world.

The Walk consists of five acres embedded with 2,400 stars, each engraved with the name of a celebrity. The five-pointed stars are made of pink terrazzo and rimmed with bronze. In addition to the honoree's name, which is inlaid in bronze, each star also has a round bronze emblem signifying the field of entertainment in which the person is best remembered. These fields are Motion Pictures, Television, Radio, Recording, and Live Theatre. The stars are surrounded by charcoal terrazzo squares.

The Walk of Fame project was conceived in the late 1950s as part of the Hollywood Improvement Program to help restore glamour to the city. Construction began in 1958, and the Walk was dedicated two years later. The first performer to receive a star was actress Joanne Woodward. New stars are added at the rate of about two per month. The Walk of Fame is one of Hollywood's most popular tourist attractions, playing host to an estimated 10 million visitors annually.

On November 16, 1999, Depp's name was added to the list of celebrities to receive a star on the Walk of Fame.

Who Cried, and *Chocolat*. When he got the opportunity to play drug smuggler George Jung in Ted Demme's *Blow*, however, he did not turn the role down. Jung was a young man who turned to trafficking in cocaine in order to fulfill his dreams of getting rich and controlling his own destiny. He was eventually captured and lost everything.

Depp met with the real-life drug smuggler several times in prison to get a better idea of the driving forces in his life. He decided that Jung "was doing what he knew best. What he got from his upbringing. He became exactly what he didn't want to be, a greedy person who doesn't think of anything other than money, just like his mother. I figured that my goal would be to take what seemed to be nothing but a party boy and turn him into a real man that you can relate to."[98]

As in several of his other movies, Depp received positive reviews for his performance in *Blow*, despite the film's generally poor reception.

More Appealing Roles

Another movie that had personal appeal for Depp was *From Hell*, based on the story of legendary nineteenth-century London killer, Jack the Ripper. As a youngster, Depp had been obsessed with the story of the Ripper. "I was always attracted to things on the darker side," said Depp, "especially when I was young…I must have 25 books on the case, maybe more. There are so many theories and any of them could be correct. It's impossible to know."[99]

From Hell opened to mixed reviews. Lou Lumenick of the *New York Post* called it "An instant classic…a gripping and stylish thriller…the classiest and best-acted slasher movie of all time."[100] Charles Taylor did not agree, proclaiming it "a brain-dead version of a dark and complex work."[101] Most, however, praised Depp's performance. Said Stacie Hougland, "The somber, serious, intense actor proves himself yet again a strong and gifted leading man, carrying off the macabre subject matter as easily as he carries off a British accent."[102]

Still another film that Depp looked forward to making was

Johnny Depp stars as Inspector Frederick Abberline in the film **From Hell.**

The Man Who Killed Don Quixote. The movie, directed by Terry Gilliam, was in the works for years. It had been plagued by a variety of problems, however, and had never been made. Depp had a personal reason for wanting to do the film. It would have paired him on the screen with Vanessa. Unfortunately, the film was never completed. Driving rains destroyed sets in Spain, another cast member was taken ill and could not continue, and financiers backing the movie had second thoughts about the project and began dropping out. Said Depp, "I hope this film [ultimately] gets made. The script is wonderful and Terry is a very innovative and wonderful director—it was just one of those things, the elements conspired against us."[103]

Following this disappointment, Depp took some time off from acting to be with his family. He worked on Vanessa's new album, called *Bliss*, and directed two of her music videos, *Pourtant* and *Que Fait La Vie*. For the most part, he just enjoyed spending time with Vanessa and Lily-Rose in the $2 million villa he had purchased in Plan-de-la-Tour in the south of France. Said Vanessa, "Johnny is the best dad. He's as good a person as he is a father."[104]

The only role that Depp accepted in 2001 was a cameo in *Once Upon A Time in Mexico*. The cameo turned into a larger role than expected, and Depp once again was the star of an otherwise lackluster film. As one of his biographers put it, "Depp is everything to the piece. He turns a brain-dead B-movie into an acceptable A-feature by his presence alone."[105]

Another Addition to the Family

Depp returned to France after shooting *Once Upon A Time in Mexico*. He wanted to spend time with Vanessa, who was pregnant with their second child. On April 9, 2002, she gave birth to a son, John Christopher Depp III.

Depp once again jumped at the role of devoted parent. Describing a typical day, he said, "I get up and make a bottle of milk up for my son and then breakfast for my girls. Then we wander out into the countryside—we live in the middle of nowhere. We might come back to the house and paint and play in the sand

Clockwise from left, Freddie Highmore, Joe Prospero, Johnny Depp, Nick Roud, Kate Winslet and Luke Spill co-star in Marc Forster's film Finding Neverland. *For this role, Depp was nominated for best actor in a leading role for the 2005 Oscars.*

box or on the swings. And in the evening I drink wine, drink coffee and go to sleep. That's my day and I love it."[106]

The birth of his son, whom they call Jack, had another effect on Depp. This one concerned his career. He decided that he wanted to make movies that his children would be able to see and enjoy. "I want to do kiddie movies now," he said. "I'm fed up with adult movies—most of them stink… since having kids and watching lots of animated cartoons and all those great old Disney films, I think they're better, they're much better. They're more fun and they take more risks."[107]

Depp's first such role was that of *Peter Pan* author, J.M. Barrie in *Finding Neverland*. "Playing Barrie was something I think I could only have done at this point in my life," he said, "because I was seeing life from an entirely fresh perspective as a parent."[108]

Depp's performance in *Finding Neverland* earned him an Academy Award nomination for Best Actor. So would his next role, that of Captain Jack Sparrow.

Captain Jack

Just as having children brought about a dramatic change in Depp's personal life, so, too, did his role in *Pirates of the Caribbean: The Curse of the Black Pearl* produce such a change in his acting career. The movie was based on the popular Disney theme park ride.

Depp was surprised, but pleased, that he was offered the role of Captain Jack Sparrow, saying,

Isn't it every boy's dream to be a pirate and get away with basically everything? Who wouldn't want to play a pirate? When I was first offered the role, I thought it was a joke. Why would Disney want to cast me? I was more shocked than anyone…. It would be nice to have a hugely successful film…especially one that you did because you loved doing it. I don't get offered too many.[109]

Of course, Depp still brought his own inimitable style to the part. He modeled his character on elements taken from rock star Keith Richards and cartoon character Pepe Le Pew. His interpretation, however, caused some concern among Disney studio executives. "There were a couple of high-end Disney executives who were fine with what I was doing," said Depp. "But there were a couple who were very worried. You know, like, 'He's ruining the movie! Why is he acting like that? What's he doing with his hand? Is the character a complete homosexual?' There was a lot of that going on for a solid month and a half. And I understood their worries, but I felt so in tune with this character and so confident that what I was doing was right that I had to say, 'Look, I understand your fear. But you've hired me to do a job. You know what I've done before, so you know it's going to be something

Pirates of the Caribbean Attraction

The *Pirates of the Caribbean* movies are based on the Disneyland attraction of the same name. Similar attractions can be found at Walt Disney World (Florida), Tokyo Disneyland, and Disneyland Park (Paris).

The original ride, designed in part by Walt Disney himself, opened in the New Orleans Square area of Disneyland on March 18, 1967. As many as 3,400 visitors an hour can ride through the attraction on water-propelled boats. They ride down a waterfall past Audio-Animatronics animated robotic figures that depict scenes aboard a pirate ship and in a burning town, all the while being serenaded by the theme song, "Yo Ho (A Pirate's Life for Me)." The ride is fifteen-and-a-half minutes long and is one of the most popular attractions in the park.

Over the years, the ride has undergone several changes. The most recent have incorporated figures from the movies. Captain Jack Sparrow, Hector Barbossa, and Davy Jones can all be seen in the current attraction.

Johnny Depp's portrayal of the iconic Captain Jack Sparrow in the **Pirates of the Caribbean** *movies is perhaps his most memorable role.*

along these lines. So please trust me. And if you can't trust me then you probably should replace me."[110]

Luckily for everyone involved, producer Jerry Bruckheimer stood behind Depp. About Depp he said,

Johnny's known for creating his own characters. He had a definite vision for Jack Sparrow which is completely unique. We just let him go and he came up with this off-center, yet very shrewd pirate. He can't quite hold his balance, his speech is a bit slurred, so you assume he's either drunk, seasick or he's been on a ship too long. But it's all an act

Keith Richards

Johnny Depp's characterization of Captain Jack Sparrow is largely based on legendary guitar player Keith Richards of the rock band The Rolling Stones. Richards had a cameo in *Pirates of the Caribbean: At World's End*, playing Sparrow's father, Captain Teague.

Richards has built a reputation for his innovative rhythm guitar work. In 2003, *Rolling Stone* magazine ranked him tenth on its list of the "100 Greatest Guitarists of All Time." Richards has also written dozens of Rolling Stones hits, many in collaboration with Mick Jagger. He was inducted into the Songwriters Hall of Fame in 1993.

Like Depp, Richards has earned a large degree of notoriety for events in his personal life, particularly with regard to alcohol and drugs. He has been arrested on drug-related charges five times.

Johnny Depp based his characterization of Captain Jack Sparrow on Keith Richards.

perpetrated for effect. And strange as it seems, it's also part of Captain Jack's charm.[111]

Box Office Hits

Pirates of the Caribbean: The Curse of the Black Pearl was released in July 2003 to mixed reviews. Depp's performance, however, was almost universally acclaimed. Wrote Ann Hornaday of *The Washington Post*, "Depp is the single best reason to see *Pirates of the Caribbean* if you're past the age of ten."[112]

Moviegoers flocked to theaters everywhere, and the film was a box office hit. It was easily Depp's most commercially successful film, tripling the box office take of his next most successful movie, *Sleepy Hollow*. It became a worldwide phenomenon and thus far has spawned three sequels.

Pirates of the Caribbean: Dead Man's Chest (2006) and *Pirates of the Caribbean: At World's End* (2007) both received negative reviews from critics. Sean Axmaker called *Dead Man's Chest* "pure cinematic junk food, a big, silly summer blockbuster whipped up from virtually nothing."[113] Still, it became the highest-grossing film of 2006—in just two weeks!

At World's End fared no better with members of the media. Poor reviews did not prevent people from going to see it, however. It grossed nearly $115 million over its opening weekend at the box office.

Many people felt Depp had become like many other actors, accepting parts in the two sequels only to cash in on Jack Sparrow's popularity. Depp disagreed. "I wanted to be Captain Jack again," he said, "because he's so much fun to play. There's so much more to explore. If they want to do *Pirates* 6 and 7, I'm there, why not?"[114]

Chapter 6

An Incredible Ride

Johnny Depp's life has been an interesting journey, taking him from Kentucky to Florida to California to France. He has been successful in his career by staying true to what he believes. "I think everybody's weird," he says, "and that's the key to it. We should celebrate our individuality, not be embarrassed or ashamed of it. We all have idiosyncrasies…people do themselves a great disservice by not allowing themselves to see who they really are because they are afraid."[115]

Recent Projects

Just because Depp had turned his attention to movies his children could eventually enjoy watching did not mean that he was completely abandoning the more unconventional projects on which he had built his reputation. His roles since the first *Pirates* movie have included a writer stalked by his alter ego (*Secret Window*), a notorious seventeenth-century poet (*The Libertine*), a voiceover for an animated young man who marries a dead woman (*Corpse Bride*), and a legendary American bank robber (*Public Enemies*).

Since making Jack Sparrow a household name, Depp's name in a movie has generally assured it of box office—if not critical—success. Recent hits include a pair of Tim Burton movies, *Charlie and the Chocolate Factory* and *Alice in Wonderland*.

In *Charlie and the Chocolate Factory*, Depp played the role

Alice in Wonderland, starring Johnny Depp as the Mad Hatter, was a top box office hit in 2010, taking in more than $116 million over its opening weekend.

of an eccentric candy maker who invites five children to tour his chocolate factory. The film was the 7th-top-grossing movie of 2005. The 2010 movie *Alice in Wonderland* was an even bigger box office hit. It took in more than $116 million in its opening weekend and ranked near the peak on the list of top-grossing movies of the year. Part of the movie's popularity and success was no doubt due to the fact that it was filmed in 3-D, making Depp's portrayal of the Mad Hatter even more memorable.

In late 2010 Depp starred in *The Tourist*, a romantic spy drama costarring Angelina Jolie. The movie, set in Paris and Venice, is loosely based on the French thriller, *Anthony Zimmer*. Depp plays an American who gets involved with an Interpol agent (Jolie). Director Florian Henckel von Donnersmarck was happy to pair up the two cinematic superstars for the first time. "They just got along so well from the first moment they met," he said, "that I knew it was going to be a lot of fun making this film."[116] After viewing the trailer for the film, Amy Kaufman of the *Los Angeles Times* was also hopeful. "The two are a great match," she wrote, "so we're optimistic that their performances can elevate the movie above the sea of other crime thrillers with guy-falls-for-spy plot lines we've seen in recent years."[117] Both Depp and Jolie were nominated for Golden Globes for their performances in *The Tourist*.

Johnny Depp meets fans on location for **The Tourist** *at Piazza San Marco in Venice, Italy.*

In 2011 Depp brought his talents to the big screen in the animated children's movie *Rango*. Depp voices the lead character, Rango, a lizard who is suddenly thrust into the role of hero when a group of bandits threaten a small Western town. Other movies scheduled for 2011 included *The Rum Diary*, based on the novel by Hunter S. Thompson; and *Pirates of the Caribbean: On Stranger Tides*.

Infinitum Nihil

Depp has long been interested in the production end of the movie industry as well as the acting side. In 2004, he founded his own production company. He called it Infinitum Nihil, meaning "Infinite Nothing." The name is taken from a line in *A Confession*, by Leo Tolstoy. The quote reads, "force is force…matter is matter…will is will…the infinite is the infinite…nothing is nothing."[118] Depp loves the name. "The beauty of it is," he says, "when someone asks you what it means, you can say, 'absolutely nothing.' Because in Latin that's what it essentially means: absolutely nothing."[119]

Depp is the company's chief executive officer (CEO). He also stars in and produces some of its films. His sister, Christie Dembrowski, serves as the firm's president, and Sam Sarkar as senior development and production executive. Infinitum Nihil entered into a working arrangement with Graham King's Initial Entertainment Group, a company that acquires and produces films. King's company is perhaps best known for the 2006 Academy Award-winning movie, *The Departed*.

Infinitum Nihil purchased the film rights to several books. The first to go into production was *The Rum Diary*, based on the novel by Hunter S. Thompson. There had been two previous unsuccessful attempts to bring the book to film prior to its purchase by Infinitum Nihil. The book describes the exploits of an American journalist who travels to Puerto Rico to write for a small Puerto Rican newspaper. The role of the journalist is Depp's second starring role in a movie based on Thompson's work.

Among other projects at different stages of development as of early 2011 are the following novels: *The Invention of Hugo Cabret*, by Brian Selznick; *Attica*, by Garry Kilworth; *The Articles of War*, by Nick Arvin; *Caliber*, by Sam Sarkar; *Fierce Invalids Home from Hot Climates*, by Tom Robbins; *The Hand of Dante*, by Nick Tosches; *Happy Days*, by Laurent Graff; *Inamorata*, by Joseph Gangemi; and *Shantaram*, by Gregory David Roberts.

Other projects include a film about the Iraq nuclear weapons program (*The Bomb in My Garden*), the story of Transylvanian bank robber Attila Ambrus (*Ballad of the Whiskey Robber*), and a film version of a popular Gothic soap opera of the late 1960s (*Dark Shadows*).

Outside Interests

Over the past few years, Depp has disposed of some of his investments. Several years ago, he sold his interest in the Parisian res-

Dark Shadows

One of the projects Infinitum Nihil tentatively scheduled for 2011 is the movie *Dark Shadows*, a groundbreaking Gothic soap opera that ran on ABC-TV for 1,225 episodes from June 27, 1966, to April 2, 1971. After a slow start, the show gained in popularity when an element of the supernatural was introduced about six months into its run. When actor Jonathan Frid joined the cast, playing the 200-year-old vampire Barnabas Collins, the show became hugely popular. Over the years, the show featured such characters as ghosts, witches, werewolves, and zombies, as well as topics such as time travel and a parallel universe.

As a youngster, Depp became obsessed with the show. He dreamed of being Barnabas Collins. He will finally get his chance, playing the character in director Tim Burton's vision of the show.

A view of the southern French town of Plan De La Tour where Johnny Depp and his long-time girlfriend Vanessa Paradis have their home.

taurant-bar Man Ray. He had been part owner in the establishment, together with actors Sean Penn and John Malkovich and singer Mick Hucknall of the band Simply Red.

Although he is no longer involved with the restaurant, Depp maintains a connection with one segment of the business. In order to celebrate the release of Vanesa's album, *Divinidylle*, in 2007, he bought his girlfriend a vineyard near their villa in Plan-de-la-Tour. A wine enthusiast, Depp has become serious about producing his homegrown vintage. Says an acquaintance, "He is very serious about his hobby and does everything himself—from selecting the grapes to working the machinery. He's done wine-tasting courses and has read virtually all there is to read on the subject. Johnny's a connoisseur."[120]

Music

Although Depp may never reach the heights he once dreamed of as a rock musician, he still takes his music seriously. "Making music is immediate," he said, "and it's all about you. If you're playing guitar, the feeling comes through the way you bend the note, the intensity with which you hit the strings. With making films, although it's real emotion, it's false emotion. You're lying."[121]

His contributions to the field have been in several different areas, including participation in film documentaries about Gypsy bands, Joe Strummer of The Clash, Tom Petty and The Heartbreakers, and The Doors. His latest music enterprise is his record label, Unison Music, which he launched in 2010. According to a source quoted in a London newspaper, "Johnny has always been passionate about music. He's taking a really hands-on approach to signing acts."[122]

Hobbies

Depp's first love has remained music. Playing guitar is not his only pastime, however. He is also an avid reader. "The best way to relax on a set," says Depp, "is to read. I just read and read and read, book after book."[123] Depp's favorite authors include Jack Kerouac, Hunter S. Thompson, Tom Robbins, Allen Ginsberg, Charles Bukowski, and William Burroughs.

Depp is also a talented artist, specializing in oil portraits. Comments Depp,

> When I can focus on something like guitar or painting, I do. I started painting people I admire, like Kerouac, Bob Dylan, Nelson Algren, Marlon Brando, Patti Smith, my girl, my kids. I painted Hunter [Thompson] a couple of times. Keith Richards. What I love to do is paint people's faces... their eyes. Because you want to find that emotion, see what's going on behind their eyes.[124]

Charity Work

Depp has donated his time and his money to many worthy causes. Charities that work with children suffering from serious diseases are particularly important to him. One of his favorites is the Children's Hospice and Palliative Care Coalition. He wears a wristband in honor of Dustin Meraz, an 11-year-old boy who died of cancer several years ago. He wore it in 2005, when he was honored with a handprint ceremony at Grauman's Chinese Theatre in Hollywood. Said Depp, "I am honored to be associ-

At his hand print ceremony at Grauman's Chinese Theatre in Hollywood, Depp wears a leather and silver wristband in honor of Dustin Meraz, an 11-year-old who died of cancer.

Johnny's Angels

Johnny Depp has donated time and money to many different charities. His efforts on the behalf of children with serious diseases are especially noteworthy.

Inspired by his charitable efforts and giving spirit, a group calling itself "Johnny's Angels: Depp Fans For Charity" was created in 2007. The group formed as a tribute to Depp for his charity work. It is staffed completely by volunteers and has no connection to him. All money raised by the group goes to Children's Hospice & Palliative Care Coalition (CHPCC), a charity that Depp also supports. Lori Butterworth and Devon Dabbs founded CHPCC in 2001 with the goal of improving care for children with life-threatening conditions and their families.

ated with brave little Dustin by wearing this silver and leather wristband."[125]

Other charities and foundations for which Depp has also helped raise money include Children in Need, Children's Hospital Los Angeles, Helen & Douglas House, Sophie's Gift, War Child, and Ronald McDonald House Charities. In March 2007, he donated $2 million to the Great Ormond Street Hospital in London, where his daughter was treated for an *E. coli* infection that affected her kidneys. She was struck down just as he was to start filming *Sweeney Todd*.

His daughter's illness gave Depp and Vanessa a great scare. "It was a reminder to us of how lucky we are," he said, "to be able to breathe, walk, talk, think and surround ourselves with people we love."[126]

In October 2006, Depp received the "Courage to Care Award" for his charity work. Said Giselle Fernandez-Farrand, organizer of the event and a member of the Children's Hospital Los Angeles Board of Trustees, "Johnny embodies the very spirit of the 'Courage to Care' Award because he puts smiles on the faces of thousands of children through his great work on film, and his longtime private advocacy of children and children's charities is nothing short of inspirational."[127]

The Family Man

Having had a bad experience with marriage at a young age, Depp has never taken that next big step, despite engagements to Sherilyn Fenn, Winona Ryder, Jennifer Grey, and Kate Moss. He has left that possibility open for Vanessa, however. Said Depp, "It would be a shame to ruin her last name. It's so perfect. It would be such a drag to stick her with Paradis-Depp.... She's the woman in my life. If she ever said, 'Hey, let's get hitched!', I'd do it in a second."[128]

A Controversial Interview

Becoming a family man has not kept Depp out of the limelight. In 2003, he again made tabloid headlines. This time, however, it was not because of his temper. It was because of something he reportedly said in an interview for the German magazine *Stern*, which quoted him as saying that "America is dumb. It's like a dumb puppy that has big teeth that can bite and hurt you, aggressive."[129]

Depp was upset, saying the quote had been taken out of context. According to Depp,

> What I was saying was that, compared to Europe, America is a very young country and we are still growing as a nation. My deepest apologies to those who were offended, affected, or hurt by this insanely twisted deformation of my words and intent...I am an American. I love my country and have great hopes for it. It is for this reason that I speak candidly and sometimes critically about it. I have benefited greatly from the freedom that exists in my country and for this I am eternally grateful.[130]

An Island Retreat

In 2004, Depp purchased a 45-acre island, called Little Hall's Pond Cay, in the Bahamas. The island is a retreat where he and his family can escape from the everyday stresses of living in the real world. "I don't think I'd ever seen any place so pure and beautiful," he said. "You can feel your pulse rate drop about 20 beats. It's instant freedom. And that rare beast—simplicity—can be had. And a little morsel of anonymity."[131]

The island is in the Exuma Land and Sea Park. Established in 1958, it is the world's first such protected reserve. Depp is determined that it shall remain that way. "Nobody is going to ever ruin the Land and Sea Park," he says. "It's like a rare gem, a diamond. I look forward to my kids growing up on the island, spending months out of the year here…learning about sea life and how to

The Imaginarium of Doctor Parnassus

Johnny Depp had an unexpected role in Terry Gilliam's 2009 fantasy, *The Imaginarium of Doctor Parnassus*. Actor Heath Ledger was one of the stars of the film. Tragically, he died in January 2008, midway through the filming.

Rather than stop production, Gilliam vowed to finish the movie and dedicate it to Ledger. As a tribute to their friend, Depp, Jude Law, and Colin Farrell all agreed to take parts in the film, each playing an incarnation of Ledger's character. Since Depp was involved in the production of *Public Enemies* at the time, he could only devote two days to the shooting of *Imaginarium*. All shots in which he was involved had to be completed in one take.

The Imaginarium of Doctor Parnassus was released in 2009 and nominated for a pair of Academy Awards. Depp, Law, and Farrell each donated their pay from the film to Ledger's 2-year-old daughter, Matilda.

protect sea life…and *their* kids growing up here, and so on."[132]

Depp and his family reach the island hideaway on a 156-foot yacht he bought and outfitted with a pirate theme, complete with the Jolly Roger, the iconic image of a skull and crossbones. The ship is the *Vajoliroja*. The name comes from the first letters of the names of each Depp family member: "VA" for Vanessa, "JO" for Depp, "LIRO" for Lily-Rose, and "JA" for Jack. The yacht is equipped with state-of-the-art technology, as well as speedboats, kayaks, water skis, wakeboards, and windsurfing and snorkeling gear.

Awards and Honors

Awards and honors have never meant much to Depp. "Sure, I find it touching, honestly," he once said, "but awards are not as important to me as when I meet a 10-year-old kid who says, 'I love Captain Jack Sparrow'… That's real magic for me."[133]

Depp has won several awards for his acting over the course of his career. He has been nominated ten times for a Golden Globe Award, which are awarded each year by members of the Hollywood Foreign Press Association. He won in 2007 for Best Performance by an Actor in a Motion Picture in a Comedy or Musical for *Sweeney Todd: The Demon Barber Of Fleet Street*, in which he played a murderous barber. Directed by Tim Burton, Depp and Burton combined to work their magic in this film that Geoff Berkshire of *Metromix* described as "an unconventional musical with rich themes, gorgeous execution and exceptional performances."[134]

One accolade that has evaded Depp thus far is the prestigious Academy Award, voted on by the actors, writers, and executives in the movie industry who are members of the American Academy of Motion Picture Arts and Sciences. He received Best Actor nominations three times, for *Pirates of the Caribbean: The Curse of the Black Pearl* (2003), *Finding Neverland* (2004), and *Sweeney Todd: The Demon Barber of Fleet Street* (2007). Just being nominated for such an award surprised Depp. As he said after receiving word of his 2003 nomination, "It was such a shock, to get the news that

Johnny Depp has been a fan favorite at the People's Choice Awards over the years, and he repays his fans by showing up to accept his awards. Here, Depp accepts the 2011 Favorite Movie Actor award.

I'd been nominated. My first reaction was: 'Why?' On one level I was flattered; but it's not what I'm working for."[135]

One of the honors with the most meaning for him is the People's Choice Award. The nominees and winners are determined by the fans rather than by industry insiders. He has been the recipient of several of these awards, including one in 2010 as the Actor of the Decade. In accepting the award, he said, "I'm deeply humbled by this great honor, which comes from you the people, which means everything to me, certainly.... Because the only reason that any of us are up here, is because of you, so thank you for that.... It has been quite an amazing decade, incredible ride, and I sincerely thank you all for bestowing upon me all your great treasures."[136]

Fans

Depp has always been quick to acknowledge that his fans are responsible for his success. He never fails to thank them publicly when he receives an award. His accessibility to those seeking

Johnny Depp never shies away from his fans, crediting them for his success.

an autograph is legendary. Says Steve Cyrkin, editor and publisher of *Autograph Magazine*, "Whether at a premiere, in a restaurant or on location, Depp may just be the best Hollywood autograph signer of all time."[137]

At the London premier of *Public Enemies*, Depp spent an hour giving autographs to fans. While many celebrities shy away from such things, he feels it is his obligation. "It's the smallest way of saying, 'Thank you,' to the people who keep not only me employed, but all of us employed, these people who go and see the film, these people who tune into the programs. That's the least I can do."[138]

Such an attitude has cemented Depp's popularity with movie-goers everywhere. He has come a long way from Owensboro, Kentucky, and has traveled what he describes as an "incredible ride."[139] He has a job for which he is "paid insane amounts of money to make different faces and tell lies pretending to be some-one else."[140]

Most importantly, he has the family he has always wanted. As Depp says, "I don't have to close my eyes to see [my dream life] because I live with it every day—with my kids, my girl, and my life. It's as perfect as it could possibly be."[141]

Introduction: The Reluctant Superstar

1. Quoted in Sean Smith, "A Pirate's Life," *Newsweek*, June 26, 2006. http://interview.johnnydepp-zone2.com/2006_0626Newsweek .html
2. Video, *Johnny Depp Dishes Dillinger with Kevin Frazier,* June 18, 2009. http://www.etonline.com/news/2009/06/75475/index.html

Chapter 1: Searching for Direction

3. Quoted in Sean Smith, "A Pirate's Life."
4. Quoted in Hilary de Vries, "The Normalization of Johnny Depp," *Los Angeles Times,* December 12, 1993. http://articles.latimes. com/1993-12-12/entertainment/ca-1173_1_depp-s-sunset-strip-johnny-depp-eating-gilbert-grape
5. Quoted in Kevin Sessums, "Johnny Be Good," *Vanity Fair,* February 1997. http://interview.johnnydepp-zone2.com/1997_02VanityFair .html
6. Quoted in Christopher Heard (ed.), *Johnny Depp Photo Album,* Plexus Publishing Limited, London, England, 2009, p.11.
7. Quoted in Cindy Pearlman, "Here's Johnny!" *Model Magazine,* December 1988. http://www.johnnydeppfan.com/interviews/model .htm
8. Quoted in Christopher Heard, *Depp,* ECW Press, Toronto, Canada, 2001, p.4.
9. Quoted in Gavin Edwards, "Johnny Depp Sings," *Rolling Stone,* January 24, 2008.
10. Quoted in Bridget Freer, "The Outsider," *FHM,* December 1998. http://interview.johnnydepp-zone2.com/1998_12FHM.html
11. Quoted in Michael Blitz and Louise Krasniewicz, *Johnny Depp: A Biography,* Greenwood Press, Westport, CT, 2008, p.65.
12. Quoted in Steve Pond, "Depp Perception," *US,* June 26, 1989. http://interview.johnnydepp-zone2.com/1989_06US.html
13. Video, *Inside the Actor's Studio – Johnny Depp 1,* September 8, 2002. http://www.youtube.com/watch?v=Jt0eqVAwhP8
14. Quoted in John Waters, "Johnny Depp," *Interview Magazine,* April 1990. http://interview.johnnydepp-zone2.com/1990_04Interview .html
15. Quoted in Holly Millea, "Ghost in the Machine: Now You See Johnny

Depp, Now You Don't," *Premiere*, February 1995. http://interview
.johnnydepp-zone2.com/1995_02Premiere.html

16. Quoted in "Biography for Johnny Depp," *Internet Movie Database.*
http://www.imdb.com/name/nm0000136/bio

17. Quoted in Brian J. Robb, *Johnny Depp: A Modern Rebel*, Plexus
Publishing Limited, London, England, 2004, pp.16-17.

18. Quoted in "A Nightmare on Elm Street – 1984 – Glen Lantz," *Depp
Impact.* http://www.deppimpact.com/nes.php

19. Quoted in Elaine Warren, "Bad Boy to Role Model," *TV
Guide,* January 23, 1988. http://interview.johnnydepp-zone2
.com/1988_0123TVGuide.html

20. Quoted in John Waters, "Johnny Depp," *Interview Magazine.*

21. Quoted in "Cute, Cool and Available! The SPLICE Interview,"
SPLICE, September 1988. http://interview.johnnydepp-zone2
.com/1988_09Splice.html

Chapter 2: The Teen Idol

22. Video, *E! True Hollywood Story: Johnny Depp – Part 1,* November 23,
2003. http://www.dailymotion.com/video/x5c30m_johnny-depp-
biography-p1-of-2_shortfilms

23. Quoted in Brian J. Robb, *Johnny Depp: A Modern Rebel,* p.21.

24. Quoted in Christopher Heard (ed.), *Johnny Depp Photo Album,*
p.19.

25. Video, *E True Hollywood Story: Johnny Depp – Part 1.*

26. Quoted in John Waters, "Johnny Depp," *Interview Magazine.*

27. Quoted in Quentin Falk & Ben Falk, *Television's Strangest Moments,*
Robson Books, London, England, 2005, p.193.

28. Quoted in Brian J. Robb, *Johnny Depp: A Modern Rebel,* p.27.

29. Quoted in Brian J. Robb, *Johnny Depp: A Modern Rebel,* p.26.

30. Quoted in Johanna Schneller, "Johnny Depp: Girls' Best Friend,"
Rolling Stone, December 1998. http://www.johnnydeppfan.com/
interviews/rs88.htm

31. Quoted in Bruno Lester, "From the Depps," *New Idea,* January 1,
2005. http://www.johnnydeppfan.com/interviews/newideajan105
.htm

32. Quoted in John Waters, "Johnny Depp," *Interview Magazine.*

33. Video, *E True Hollywood Story: Johnny Depp – Part 1.*

34. Video, *The Late Show With David Letterman (Johnny Depp) Part 1.*
http://www.youtube.com/watch?v=0R-eZt0Qvko&p=1AF7151AD
4D4D6D1&playnext=1&index=1

35. Video, *E True Hollywood Story: Johnny Depp – Part 1.*

36. Video, *E True Hollywood Story: Johnny Depp – Part 1.*

37. Quoted in Christopher Heard (ed.), *Johnny Depp Photo Album,* p.28.
38. Video, *E True Hollywood Story: Johnny Depp – Part 1.*
39. Video, *E True Hollywood Story: Johnny Depp – Part 1.*
40. Quoted in Christopher Heard, *Depp,* p.50.
41. Quoted in Christopher Heard, *Depp,* p.51.
42. Quoted in Brian J. Robb, *Johnny Depp: A Modern Rebel,* p.40.
43. Quoted in Brian J. Robb, *Johnny Depp: A Modern Rebel,* p.38.

Chapter 3: Ups and Downs

44. Quoted in Mark Salisbury (ed.), *Burton on Burton,* Faber and Faber Limited, London, England, 1995, p.87.
45. Quoted in Michael Blitz and Louise Krasniewicz, *Johnny Depp: A Biography,* p.35-36.
46. Quoted in Mark Salisbury (ed.), *Burton on Burton,* p.xi.
47. Quoted in Mark Salisbury (ed.), *Burton on Burton,* pp.92-93.
48. Quoted in Christopher Heard (ed.), *Johnny Depp Photo Album,* p.39.
49. Quoted in Brian J. Robb, *Johnny Depp: A Modern Rebel,* p.66.
50. Quoted in Janet Maslin, "He's His Sister's Keeper, and What a Job That Is," *The New York Times,* April 16, 1993.
51. Quoted in Brian J. Robb, *Johnny Depp: A Modern Rebel,* p.55.
52. Quoted in Brian J. Robb, *Johnny Depp: A Modern Rebel,* p.70.
53. Quoted in Holly Millea, "Ghost in the Machine: Now You See Johnny Depp, Now You Don't," *Premiere.*
54. Quoted in Dan Yakir, "Truly Madly Depply," *Sky Magazine,* April 1994.
55. Quoted in Christopher Heard (ed.), *Johnny Depp Photo Album,* p.44.
56. Quoted in Hilary de Vries, "The Normalization of Johnny Depp," *Los Angeles Times.*
57. Quoted in Michael Blitz and Louise Krasniewicz, *Johnny Depp: A Biography,* pp.43-44.
58. Quoted in Hilary de Vries, "The Normalization of Johnny Depp," *Los Angeles Times.*
59. Quoted in Hilary de Vries, "The Normalization of Johnny Depp," *Los Angeles Times.*
60. Quoted in "Quotes by Johnny Depp," *In A Depp Trance.* http://inadepptrance.com/Quotes-AA-Johnny's.htm
61. Quoted in Holly Millea, "Ghost in the Machine: Now You See Johnny Depp, Now You Don't," *Premiere.*

Chapter 4: Oddballs, Eccentrics and Outcasts

62. Quoted in Jessica Winter, "Depp & Meaningful," *TimeOut*, April 6-13, 2005. http://www.johnnydeppfan.com/interviews/time-out040605.htm

63. Quoted in Brian J. Robb, *Johnny Depp: A Modern Rebel*, p.100.

64. Quoted in Christopher Heard (ed.), *Johnny Depp Photo Album*, p.56.

65. Quoted in Barbara Shulgasser, "At Least He's A Don Juan to Love," *San Francisco Chronicle*, April 7, 1995. http://www.sfgate.com/cgi-bin/article.cgi?f=/e/a/1995/04/07/WEEKEND8039.dtl

66. Quoted in Roger Ebert, "Don Juan DeMarco," *Chicago Sun-Times*, April 7, 1995. http://rogerebert.suntimes.com/apps/pbcs.dll/article?AID=/19950407/REVIEWS/504070304/1023

67. Quoted in Brian J. Robb, *Johnny Depp: A Modern Rebel*, p.108.

68. Quoted in Holly Millea, "Ghost in the Machine: Now You See Johnny Depp, Now You Don't," *Premiere*.

69. Quoted in Michael Blitz and Louise Krasniewicz, *Johnny Depp: A Biography*, p.53.

70. Quoted in Edward Guthmann, "'Nick of Time' Misses the Mark," *San Francisco Chronicle*, November 22, 1995. http://www.sfgate.com/cgi bin/article.cgi?f=/c/a/1995/11/22/DD44251.DTL

71. Quoted in Tara Ariano and Sarah D. Bunting, "Johnny Depp Does It Better Than Most," *Movies on Today*. http://today.msnbc.msn.com/id/6434732

72. Quoted in Bridget Freer, "The Outsider," *FHM*.

73. Quoted in Christopher Heard (ed.), *Johnny Depp Photo Album*, p.64.

74. Quoted in Christopher Heard (ed.), *Johnny Depp Photo Album*, p.66.

75. Quoted in Christopher Heard (ed.), *Johnny Depp Photo Album*, p.66.

76. Quoted in Nathan Rabin, *My Year of Flops*, Scribner, New York, 2010. http://www.avclub.com/articles/the-unseen-case-file-153-the-brave-1997,36756/

77. Video, *What's Eating Johnny Depp?*, December 30, 1998. Transcript at: http://www.johnnydeppfan.com/interviews/wejd.htm

78. Quoted in Michael Blitz and Louise Krasniewicz, *Johnny Depp: A Biography*, p.62.

79. Quoted in Michael Blitz and Louise Krasniewicz, *Johnny Depp: A Biography*, p.62.

80. Quoted in Brian J. Robb, *Johnny Depp: A Modern Rebel*, p.122.

81. Quoted in Jacques-André Bondy, "Johnny Goes to Cannes,"

Premiere, June 1998. http://jabondy.free.fr/255Depp/3UK.html

82. Quoted in Roger Ebert, "Fear And Loathing In Las Vegas," *Chicago Sun-Times,* May 22, 1998. http://rogerebert.suntimes.com/apps/pbcs.dll/article?AID=/19980522/REVIEWS/805220303/1023

83. Quoted in Christopher Heard (ed.), *Johnny Depp Photo Album,* p.74.

84. Quoted in Dustin Putman, "The Astronaut's Wife," *The Movie Boy,* August 29, 1999. http://www.themovieboy.com/reviews/a/99_astronautswife.htm

85. Quoted in John H. Richardson, "The Unprocessed Johnny Depp," *Esquire,* May 2004.

86. Quoted in James Berardinelli, "The Ninth Gate," *Reelviews.* http://www.reelviews.net/php_review_template.php?identifier=325

87. Quoted in Betty Jo Tucker, "Johnny Depp Enriches *The Ninth Gate,*" *ReelTalk.* http://www.reeltalkreviews.com/browse/viewitem.asp?type=review&id=104

88. Quoted in Kyle Smith, "Keeping His Head: Sleepy Hollow Star and New Dad Johnny Depp Settles Down—And Likes It," *People,* December 13, 1999. http://www.johnnydeppfan.com/interviews/people1299.htm

89. Quoted in Jan Janssen, "Johnny Depp: Pan Handler," *Ms London,* September 27, 2004. http://www.johnnydeppfan.com/interviews/mslondon92704.htm

Chapter 5: The Family Man

90. Quoted in Martha Frankel, "A Man Apart," *Movieline*, March 2001. http://interview.johnnydepp-zone2.com/2001_03Movieline.html

91. Quoted in "Johnny Depp Talks About The Paparazzi," *Depp Impact.* http://www.deppimpact.com/about_paparazzi.php

92. Quoted in Harold von Kursk, "Johnny Depp: 'Who Knows, Maybe I'm Becoming A Big Boy Finally,'" *Avantgarde*, September 1999. http://www.johnnydeppfan.com/interviews/avantgarde.htm

93. Quoted in Claudia Puig, "Happiness Finds Johnny Depp," *USA Today,* March 7, 2004. http://www.usatoday.com/life/people/2004-03-07-depp_x.htm

94. Quoted in Jessamy Calkin, "The Esquire Interview: Johnny Depp ESQ," *Esquire*, February 2000. http://interview.johnnydepp-zone2.com/2000_02Esquire.html

95. Quoted in Brian J. Robb, *Johnny Depp: A Modern Rebel*, p.135.

96. Transcript of audio interview, *Europe 2*, 2000. http://www.johnnydeppfan.com/interviews/europe2.htm

97. Quoted in Johanna Schneller, "Where's Johnny?" *Premiere*, December 1999. http://interview.johnnydepp-zone2.com/1999_12Premiere. html

98. Quoted in Ersie Danou, "Johnny Depp: Closer to the Light," *Cinema Magazine,* June 2001. http://www.johnnydeppfan.com/interviews/cinema601.htm

99. Quoted in Thomas Quinn, "Johnny Cool Chills Out," *The Mirror,* February 8, 2002. http://www.thefreelibrary.com/ilm%3A+JOHNNY+COOL+CHILLS+OUT%3B+Why+Johnny+Depp+turned+his+back+on...-a082635372

100. Quoted in Lou Lumenick, "Ripping Good Slasher," *New York Post,* October 19, 2001. http://www.nypost.com/p/entertainment/ripping_good_slasher_4K49bUx7xbY2FUbANNw3sJ

101. Quoted in Charles Taylor, "From Hell," *Salon.com*, October 19, 2001. http://www.salon.com/entertainment/movies/review/2001/10/19/from_hell

102. Quoted in Stacie Hougland, "From Hell," *Hollywood.com.* http://www.hollywood.com/review/From_Hell/1096583

103. Quoted in Christopher Heard (ed.), *Johnny Depp Photo Album,* p.94.

104. Quoted in Brian J. Robb, *Johnny Depp: A Modern Rebel,* p.159.

105. Quoted in Michael Blitz and Louise Krasniewicz, *Johnny Depp: A Biography,* p.79.

106. Quoted in Brian J. Robb, *Johnny Depp: A Modern Rebel,* p.165.

107. Quoted in Jessamy Calkin, "One That Got Away," *Daily Telegraph,* August 3, 2002. http://interview.johnnydepp-zone2.com/2002_0803DailyTelegraph.html

108. Quoted in Christopher Heard (ed.), *Johnny Depp Photo Album,* p.95.

109. Quoted in Brian J. Robb, *Johnny Depp: A Modern Rebel,* p.168.

110. Quoted in Chris Nashawaty, "Johnny Depp," *Entertainment Weekly,* September 19, 2003. http://www.ew.com/ew/article/0,,485218,00.html

111. Quoted in Brian J. Robb, *Johnny Depp: A Modern Rebel,* p.171.

112. Quoted in Ann Hornaday, "Depp Is the Wind in 'Pirates of Caribbean' Sails," *The Washington Post,* July 11, 2003. http://web.kitsapsun.com/redesign/2003-07-11/features/a&e/198803.shtml

113. Quoted in Sean Axmaker, "Johnny Depp and the 'Pirates 2' Crew Invite You Aboard," *Seattle Post-Intelligencer*, July 6, 2006. http://www.seattlepi.com/movies/276531_pirates06q.html

114. Quoted in Rick Fulton, "The Razz Interview: My Wonka's No Wacko; Johnny Depp Denies Basing His Weird and

Wacky Movie Character on the King of Pop," *Daily Record,* July 22, 2005. http://www.thefreelibrary.com/ the+Razz+interview%3A+My+Wonka's+no+Wacko%3B+Johnny+ Depp+denies+basing...-a0134279624

Chapter 6: An Incredible Ride

115. Quoted in Chrissy Iley, "'I Felt Weirdness for Many Years,'" *The Guardian,* July 3, 2006. http://www.interview.johnnydepp-zone2 .com/2006_0703TheGuardian.html

116. Quoted in Kara Warner, "Angelina Jolie And Johnny Depp Have 'Incredible Chemistry,' 'Tourist' Director Says," *MTV.com,* September 1, 2010. http://www.mtv.com/news/articles/1646932/20100831/ story.jhtml

117. Quoted in Amy Kaufman, "Angelina Jolie and Johnny Depp Play 'Tourist': Preview Review Trailer," *Los Angeles Times,* September 15, 2010. http://latimesblogs.latimes.com/movies/2010/09/angelina-jolie-johnny-depp-the-tourist-preview-review-trailer.html

118. Leo Tolstoy, *A Confession,* W.W. Norton & Company, Inc., 1996, p.59.

119. Quoted in Erik Hedegaard, "Johnny Darko," *Rolling Stone,* February 10, 2005. http://www.interview.johnnydepp-zone2 .com/2005_0210RollingStone.html

120. Quoted in Clemmie Moodie & Danielle Lawler, "Pirate Walks the Plonk," *The Mirror,* June 23, 2008. http://www.thefreelibrary.com/ 3am%3A+Pirate+walks+the+plonk.-a0180455120

121. Quoted in Anthony Decurtis, "Johnny Depp," *Rolling Stone 30th Anniversary Special,* 1998. http://www.johnnydeppfan.com /interviews/rollingstone.htm

122. Quoted in "Scissor Bands for Actor Depp," *The Sun,* June 19, 2010. http://www.thesun.co.uk/sol/homepage/showbiz/bizarre/ usa/3020857/Scissor-bands-for-actor-Depp-as-Pirates-Of-The-Caribbean-star-sets-up-own-music-label.html

123. Quoted in "Choc Talk," *Nickelodeon Magazine,* August 2005. http:// www.interview.johnnydepp-zone2.com/2005_08Nickelodeon .html

124. Quoted in Douglas Brinkley, "Johnny Depp's Great Escape," *Vanity Fair,* July 2009. http://www.vanityfair.com/culture/features/2009/07 /johnny-depp200907.

125. Quoted in "Johnny Depp Remembers Dustin by Wearing Leather and Silver Wrist Band," *Children's Hospice and Palliative Care Coalition.* http://www.childrenshospice.org/coalition/news/johnny-depp-dustin/

126. Quoted in Pete Norman, "Report: Johnny Depp Talks About Daughter's Illness," *People Magazine*, May 10, 2007. http://www.people.com/people/article/0,,20038452,00.html

127. Quoted in "Gala Benefit for Childrens Hospital Los Angeles Will Honor Johnny Depp, Ralph Alvarez and Others," *Globe Newswire*, October 6, 2006. http://www.globenewswire.com/newsroom/news.html?d=106431

128. Quoted in Evelyn Moore, "Johnny Depp: The Heart-Throb and Sometime Pirate On Love and the Paparazzi," *OK Magazine*, January 4, 2005. http://www.deppimpact.com/mags/ok_04jan05.php

129. Quoted in "Johnny Depp: U.S. Is Like A Stupid Puppy," *CNN*, September 3, 2003. http://www.cnn.com/2003/SHOWBIZ/Movies/09/03/depp.us.reax.reut/

130. Quoted in Gary Susman, "Depp Charge," *Entertainment Weekly*, September 5, 2003. http://www.ew.com/ew/article/0,,482664,00.html

131. Quoted in Douglas Brinkley, "Johnny Depp's Great Escape," *Vanity Fair.*

132. Quoted in Douglas Brinkley, "Johnny Depp's Great Escape."

133. Quoted in Sandra Smith, "Johnny and Jude Are the Men of the Moment," *The Guardian*, October 27, 2004. http://www.guardian.co.uk/film/2004/oct/27/features.johnnydepp

134. Quoted in Geoff Berkshire, "Sweeney Todd: The Demon Barber of Fleet Street," *Metromix,* December 21, 2007. http://chicago.metromix.com/movies/movie_review/sweeney-todd-the-demon/272243/content

135. Quoted in Erik Hedegaard, "Johnny Darko," *Rolling Stone.*

136. Video, *Johnny Depp at People's Choice Awards.* http://www.youtube.com/watch?v=W7B7CMQb-Uw

137. Quoted in "Depp Named Top Autograph Signer as Ferrell Bombs," Reuters, December 18, 2007. http://www.reuters.com/article/idUSN1434080920071218

138. Video, *Johnny Depp Interview.* http://www.youtube.com/watch?v=cwR91cc23hg

139. Video, *Johnny Depp at People's Choice Awards.*

140. Quoted in Michael Blitz and Louise Krasniewicz, *Johnny Depp: A Biography,* p.xi.

141. Quoted in Josh Young, "The Neverland Effect," *Life Magazine*, November 19, 2004. http://www.interview.johnnydepp-zone2.com/2004_1118Life.html

Books

Nigel Goodall, *The Secret World of Johnny Depp: The Intimate Biography of Hollywood's Best-Loved Rebel.* London, England: John Blake Publishing Ltd., 2010. An in-depth and candid biography of Hollywood's most famous outsider.

Christopher Heard (Ed.), *Johnny Depp Photo Album.* London, England: Plexus Publishing Limited, 2009. This paperback includes dozens of color photos and hundreds of quotes by, and about, Depp.

Nick Johnstone, *Johnny Depp: The Illustrated Biography.* London, England: Carlton Books Ltd., 2008. A lavishly illustrated biography of the charismatic Hollywood star.

Brian J. Robb, *Johnny Depp: A Modern Rebel.* London, England: Plexus Publishing Limited, 2004. A thorough biography of Depp, with special attention given to the stories behind each of his films.

Michael Singer, *Bring Me That Horizon: The Making of* Pirates of the Caribbean. Disney Editions, 2007. This book includes detailed descriptions about the making of the first three *Pirates* movies, and about the journey from a Disneyland attraction to a major motion picture.

Periodicals

Steve Daly, "Johnny Depp: Cutting Loose in *Sweeney Todd*," *Entertainment Weekly,* November 9, 2007.

Stephen Rebello, "Heeere's Johnny!", *Biography Magazine*, Fall 2004.

Sean Smith, "A Pirate's Life," *Newsweek*, June 26, 2006.

Josh Young, "The Neverland Effect," *Life Magazine*, November 19, 2004.

Websites

Depp Impact (http://www.deppimpact.com/). This fansite contains a great deal of information about each of Depp's films, including publicity photos, sound clips, and trailers.

The Internet Movie Database (http://www.imdb.com/). The place to go to find out anything and everything about your favorite movies.

Johnny Depp Zone (http://www.johnnydepp-zone.com/). One of the better-organized Depp fansites, it has an extensive collection of magazine articles and interviews.

Important Dates

1963
John Christopher Depp II is born to Betty Sue and John Depp Sr. on June 9 in Owensboro, Kentucky.

1970
Family moves to Miramar, Florida.

1975
Mother buys Depp his first guitar.

1978
Betty Sue and John Depp Sr. divorce.

1981
Joins Florida band The Kids.

1983
Marries Lori Ann Allison on December 24.
Moves to Los Angeles, California, where he works as a telemarketer.

1984
Is introduced to Nicolas Cage.
Gets first role in *A Nightmare on Elm Street,* which is released that November.

1985
Divorces Lori Anne.
Appears in student film, *Dummies.*
Begins dating actress Sherilyn Fenn.
Appears in *Private Resort.*

1986
Appears in made-for-television's *Slow Burn* and in *Platoon.*

1987
Begins role of Tom Hanson on television's *21 Jump Street,* which debuts on April 21.

1988
Breaks up with Sherilyn Fenn.

1989

Begins dating actress Jennifer Grey, gets engaged, but eventually breaks up.
Is arrested after incident in Vancouver hotel.
Begins dating actress Winona Ryder.

1990

Gets engaged to Winona Ryder.
21 Jump Street is cancelled.
Appears in *Cry-Baby* and *Edward Scissorhands*, for which he receives his
   first Golden Globe nomination.

1991

Appears in *Freddy's Dead: The Final Nightmare.*
Appears in Tom Petty and The Heartbreakers video, "Into the Great
   Wide Open."

1993

Appears in *Arizona Dream, Benny & Joon*, and *What's Eating Gilbert
   Grape?*
Breaks up with Winona Ryder.
Buys controlling interest in The Viper Room.
Actor River Phoenix dies outside The Viper Room from a drug overdose.

1994

Begins dating model Kate Moss.
Appears in *Ed Wood.*
Is arrested for disturbance at the Mark Hotel in New York.

1995

Appears in *Don Juan DeMarco, Dead Man*, and *Nick of Time.*

1997

Appears in *Donnie Brasco.*
Appears in—and directs—*The Brave.*

1998

Breaks up with Kate Moss.
Appears in *Fear and Loathing in Las Vegas* and *L.A. Without a Map.*
Begins dating singer/actress Vanessa Paradis.

1999

Is arrested for incident at Mirabelle restaurant in London.
Receives the César Award for his body of work.
Daughter Lily-Rose Melody Depp born on May 27.
Appears in *The Astronaut's Wife* and *Sleepy Hollow.*
Receives a star on the Hollywood Walk of Fame.

2000

Appears in *The Ninth Gate, Before Night Falls*, and *Chocolat*.

2001

Appears in *The Man Who Cried, Blow,* and *From Hell*.

2002

Son John Christopher Depp III born on April 9.

2003

Appears in *Once Upon a Time in Mexico* and *Pirates of the Caribbean: The Curse of the Black Pearl*, for which he receives an Academy Award nomination.

2004

Appears in *Secret Window, Finding Neverland*, and *The Libertine*.
Buys Little Hall's Pond Cay in the Bahamas.
Founds production company, Infinitum Nihil.

2005

Appears in *Charlie and the Chocolate Factory* and does a voice-over in *Corpse Bride*.

2006

Appears in *Pirates of the Caribbean: Dead Man's Chest*.
Receives Courage to Care Award.

2007

Appears in *Pirates of the Caribbean: At World's End* and *Sweeney Todd: The Demon Barber of Fleet Street,* for which he wins his first Golden Globe Award.

2009

Appears in *Public Enemies*.

2010

Appears in *Alice in Wonderland* and *The Tourist,* for which he receives a Golden Globe nomination.
Wins People's Choice Award for Favorite Movie Actor of the Decade.

2011

Voices the lead character in *Rango* and appears in *Pirates of the Caribbean: On Stranger Tides*.

Picture Credits

Cover Photo: © London Red Carpet/Alamy
AP Images/Andrew Lichtenstein, 44
AP Images/Eric Draper, 40
AP Images/Francois Mori, 60
AP Images/Kathy Willens, 53
AP Images/Luis Martinez, 79
AP Images/Matt Sayles, 9
AP Images/Reed Saxon, 62
Barbara Zanon/Getty Images, 74
© Bureau L.A. Collection/Corbis, 38
Chris Jackson/Getty Images, 27
© CinemaPhoto/Corbis, 25
© Clive Coote/Miramax Films/Bureau L.A. Collection/Corbis, 66
© Deborah Feingold/Corbis, 14
Ebet Roberts/Redferns/Getty Images, 18
© Frank Trapper/Corbis, 70
Getty Images, 47
Hulton Archive/Getty Images, 37
James Aylott/Getty Images, 50
Juergen Vollmer/Redferns/Getty Images, 65
Ke.Mazur/WireImage/Getty Images, 30
Kevin Winter/Getty Images, 84
Mike Franklin/FilmMagic/Getty Images, 17
Orion/The Kobal Collection/Francisco, Ricky, 22
© Photos 12/Alamy, 20, 31, 34, 52, 73
Ron Galella/WireImage/Getty Images, 16
SGranitz/WireImage/Getty Images, 57
Soul Brother/Getty Images, 85
Stuart Morton/Getty Images, 77
Walt Disney Pictures/The Kobal Collection, 69

About the Author

John Grabowski is a native of Brooklyn, New York. He holds a bachelor's degree in psychology from City College of New York and a master's degree in educational psychology from Teachers College, Columbia University. He was a teacher for thirty-nine years, as well as a writer, specializing in the fields of sports, education, and comedy. His body of published work includes fifty-four books; a nationally syndicated sports column; consultation on several math textbooks; articles for newspapers, magazines, and the programs of professional sports teams; and comedy material sold to Jay Leno, Joan Rivers, Yakov Smirnoff, and numerous other comics. He and his wife, Patricia, live in Staten Island with their daughter, Elizabeth.